THE CUTTING **EDGE**

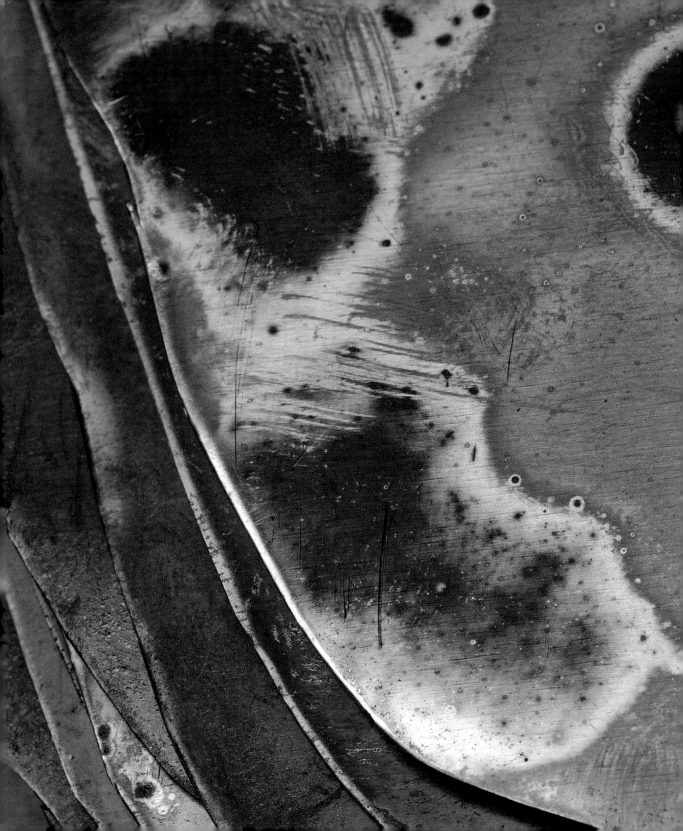

THE CUTTING EDGE

SCOTLAND'S CONTEMPORARY CRAFTS

EDITED BY

Catriona Baird and Rose Watban

PHOTOGRAPHS BY

Shannon Tofts

Published by
NMS Enterprises Limited – Publishing
National Museums Scotland
Chambers Street
Edinburgh EH1 1JF

Text
© Individual essays and contributions as credited 2007

All photographs © Shannon Tofts 2007

Copyright of completed work photographed in this book remains
with the makers as credited.

Publication format by
NMS Enterprises Limited – Publishing
© Trustees of the National Museums of Scotland 2007

BRITISH LIBRARY CATALOGUING IN PUBLICATION DATA
A catalogue record for this book
is available from the British Library

10 digit ISBN: 1 905267 07 X
13 digit ISBN: 978 1 905267 07 1

Book layout and design by Mark Blackadder
Cover based on design by NMS Design; cover image shows copper sheets,
    raw material for the work of Rachel Hazell; photograph by Shannon Tofts

Published with support from National Museums Scotland

www.nms.ac.uk

Printed and bound in the United Kingdom by Cambridge Printing

CONTENTS

PREFACE

The Cutting Edge realizes a long held ambition for a contemporary craft exhibition to highlight the strong and diverse new work, often led from within the applied arts departments of Scotland's colleges of art, emerging from the harnessing of new technologies and the integration of digital and hand techniques. The exhibition follows on from *Celebrating Scotland's Crafts*, National Museums Scotland's immensely popular touring exhibition (2000-03) which was supported by the Scottish Arts Council and showcased the contemporary practice of Scotland's rich indigenous crafts traditions.

The Cutting Edge is the product of a collaboration between Aberdeen City Council, East Ayrshire Council, Glasgow City Council and National Museums Scotland. This sharing of expertise and resources has allowed the creation of a major show which will both be seen across Scotland and provide a vehicle for promoting Scottish talent abroad.

The Scottish Arts Council has been pleased to support this initiative from its early stages as part of our commitment to enabling audiences in Scotland to see and enjoy the best of contemporary crafts. We wish *The Cutting Edge* every success.

Dr Helen Bennett
HEAD OF CRAFTS
Scottish Arts Council

FOREWORD

The aim of *The Cutting Edge* is to present the best of modern Scottish crafts to wide-ranging and diverse audiences across Scotland. To do this, staff from four organisations – Aberdeen City Council, East Ayrshire Council, Glasgow City Council and National Museums Scotland – have worked together in partnership to develop the exhibition and this accompanying publication. The exhibition is launched in Edinburgh at the National Museum of Scotland, before touring to each of the partner's venues, and then on to a national and international tour during 2007 and 2008.

The word 'crafts' is often associated with ideas of tradition and heritage. Whilst many of today's craft-makers undoubtedly are influenced by their ancestral roots, by a continuing preoccupation with the recurring themes of Scottish art and psyche, and by traditional techniques, *The Cutting Edge* clearly demonstrates the wealth of well-designed, beautiful and brilliantly-made objects in modern-day Scotland. All the work in this exhibition is by Scottish makers, showcasing what they are making now. Thirty makers have participated in the project, nine of whom were commissioned by selection process to create new work as a lasting legacy. All responded magnificently to the double meaning of the brief by creating work that is both innovative and uses cutting tools in its creation. We are privileged in Scotland to have a strong creative crafts community and we wish to extend our heartfelt thanks to all the makers participating in this project.

Working in partnership brings many new challenges and opportunities. This partnership began after the success of *Fired With Colour* (2000), which told the story of enamelling in Britain and set contemporary enamel practice in context. *Fired With Colour* was developed by curators at Aberdeen Art Gallery & Museums and the now National Museums Scotland, joined by The Scottish Gallery. At the conclusion of the exhibition the organisers were agreed that the benefits of working together were immense, in spite of the geographical challenges. From these beginnings *The Cutting Edge* was developed by National Museums Scotland, now working with colleagues in Aberdeen, East Ayrshire and Glasgow.

Each of the partners has a strong commitment to developing and presenting crafts, with projects including Develop Craft Ayrshire, the Aberdeen Metalwork Collection formed with support from the National Collecting Scheme for Scotland, new commissions for Glasgow Museums, and a sustained exhibition programme at National Museums Scotland. By sharing our resources and expertise we have been able to realize our aims, which the partner organisations would not have been able to achieve individually.

We are particularly grateful for the financial support given to the project by the Scottish Arts Council National Lottery Fund. Without this funding it would have been impossible to create the exhibition. We would also like to express our thanks for the support and advice from Dr Helen Bennett and Clare Hanna of the Scottish Arts Council Crafts Department.

We are delighted that both Grace Cochrane and David McFadden have contributed informative essays on aspects of Scottish craft from an international perspective, and we are indebted to Philippa Swann and Simon Olding for their fascinating contributions on the United Kingdom perspective. We also wish to extend sincere thanks to Shannon Tofts for his thoughtful and illuminating photographs and maker portraits.

The Cutting Edge has taken more than three years to develop; throughout this time we have had the joy of working with Catriona Baird, who as Exhibition Project Curator has shown tremendous organisational skills and remarkable patience with our foibles. Without Catriona's support and dedication our task of presenting this show would have been extremely difficult.

Working on *The Cutting Edge* has been an immensely rewarding experience for all the partners and it is our aspiration that it will be the catalyst for a new appreciation and understanding of Scotland's makers and their skills.

Phillipa Aitken, Christine Rew, Rose Watban, Rosemary Watt
JANUARY 2007

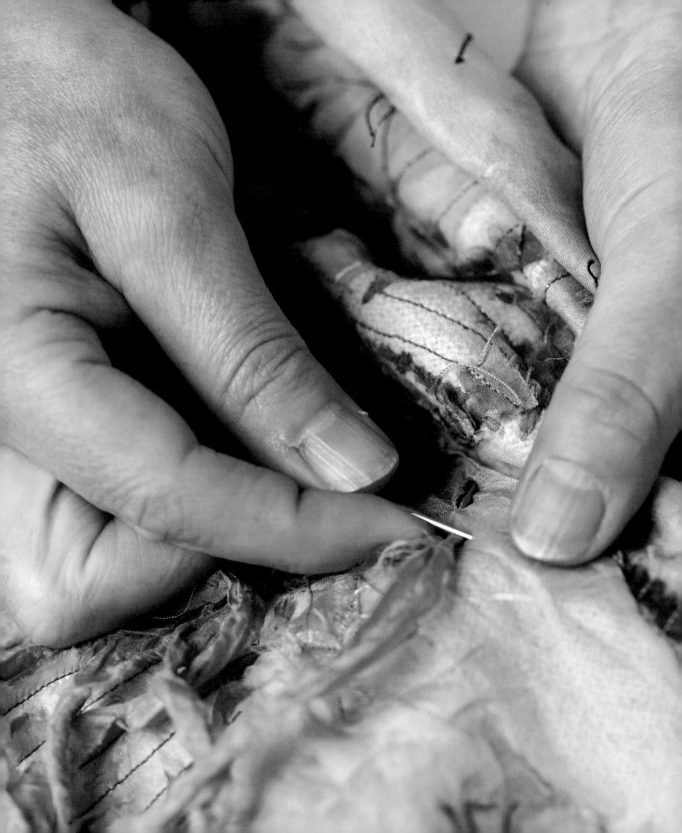

A PERSPECTIVE ON
SCOTTISH CONTEMPORARY CRAFTS

Philippa Swann

From its northerly position, Scotland may seem on the geographic margins of mainstream contemporary British crafts, but given the increasing globalization of all things cultural it is interesting to consider whether there is a boundary, a coherent Scottish 'style'. *The Cutting Edge* aims to deliver the best of Scottish contemporary crafts, and while not absolutely definitive in its selection, what it presents certainly offers an insight to the country's distinctive applied arts scene.

Attempts to analyse a national school are fraught with inconsistencies. Where you have diversity – and *The Cutting Edge* reveals works of ingenious technical wizardry, irreverent and provocative subject matter, restrained abstractions, colourful and outrageous excess, designer interior chic, nature and whimsy – you have multi-layered complexity. Moreover, there's a voice in my head, straight out of Kathleen Jamie's poem 'Arraheids',[1] that constantly warns me about my task. This is the voice of self-appointed authority, reminding me of that typical Scottish view that you should not get too carried away with imaginative flights of fancy. Here are objects made of metal, glass, textile, willow and plastic that may have undergone fabulous transformations in the process of creation, but where do they fit into the bigger picture of contemporary culture?

Surprisingly, Scottish contemporary crafts have barely penetrated public awareness; the result, no doubt, of a kind of collective reticence – a national failure to blow one's own trumpet. This has been my observation of the past 15 years working first at Edinburgh College of Art and more recently as contributing editor for *Crafts* magazine. I also live and work with engraver Malcolm Appleby and witness frequently the astonishment expressed by people encountering his work for the first time. Among Appleby's extensive output is his extraordinary silver assemblage inspired by Scotland's coastline that forms the table-centre for the Millennium Collection for Bute House. Designed for use at the official residence of Scotland's First Minister, the Bute Collection was the initiative of the Incorporation of Goldsmiths of the City of Edinburgh and marked the return of a Parliament to Scotland and the new Millennium. The other silversmiths exhibiting in *The Cutting Edge* – Adrian Hope, Michael Lloyd and Grant McCaig – contributed the cutlery, water jugs and fruit bowl respectively to the collection, creating one-off pieces that epitomized their own individual approach to metal. The Bute Collection is unquestionably 'a definitive statement of silversmithing in Scotland at the beginning of the 21st century'[2] and celebrates national optimism through objects that are both functional and eloquent.

On another level, I experienced a profound sense of marvel when I encountered the brilliance of Peter Chang's work for the first time. Chang makes 'indefinable objects which are both sculpture and jewellery'[3] and he was commissioned to create an architectural piece for ART™, an Inverness gallery renovated in 1998. His outrageously otherworldly handrail, like a fossil fragment of a dragon's wing, perches upon the lower staircase at ART™. Critic Rosemary Hill wrote of Chang's work, 'these strange forms reverberate in our imaginations',[4] and for artistic shock value nothing can compare with his vibrant colours and audacious forms, inspired by extreme nature, camouflage and warning, installed fearlessly within this seemingly conservative Highland town.

Chang was winner of the 1995 Jerwood Prize for Jewellery and he is internationally renowned for his masterful use of fabricated plastic. His work highlights the fact that contemporary jewellery has long since eschewed conventional materials, methods and subject matter, while taking traditional practices to new dimensions.

The ground-breaking and popular exhibition *Jewellery Moves*, an expansive exposition of around 400 pieces from 24 countries, at the Royal Museum (now National Museum of Scotland) in 1999, drew attention to the extraordinary range of international studio work and helped to reinforce jewellery's place 'on the contemporary cultural map of Scotland'.[5]

Scottish studio jewellery has achieved a well-earned international reputation due to the strength of its established practitioners and also the excellence of

its degree level courses. Scottish art colleges have long been held in high esteem and places on jewellery and silversmithing courses are in demand. Teachers such as jewellers Dorothy Hogg, Jack Cunningham and Roger Morris have not only left their personal stamp on the sector, but maintained a high level of personal practice (both Hogg and Cunningham were shortlisted for the 2000 Jerwood Prize). Scottish jewellery degree shows are exhilarating occasions and a chance to see risk-taking, originality and experimentation. What specially marks Scottish jewellery is the confidence of emerging makers, rarely imitative, but endlessly imaginative. This can be seen in the creative individualism and the variety of approaches to materials and techniques in *The Cutting Edge's* jewellers.

Hogg has been Head of Edinburgh College of Art's Jewellery and Silver-smithing Department for more than 20 years, and she has been a particularly influential teacher. Hogg's work is remarkable in its deceptively restrained simplicity. Exploring what she calls 'opposing forces',[6] Hogg combines intellectual formality with a human quality, drawing on ineffably sensual effects – movement, sound, a hint of colour. Her preference for precious metals alongside what writer Marina Vaizey describes as 'intuitive geometry',[7] leads to forms that are both expressive and abstract. In Hogg's work, moreover, we catch glimpses of minimalism, one of the characteristic elements of Scottish visual art.

Edinburgh graduate Andrew Lamb has already made considerable waves with his distinctive work in gold and silver wire since leaving the Royal College of Art in 2004. Lamb's interest is visual effects – the subtle way surfaces change with movement. His collection, appropriately called *Seeing is Believing*, is inspired by the illusions created by *moiré* and *ikat* textiles, or of those found in nature, such as animal markings. It is tempting to connect Lamb's preoccupation with surface illusion with that strand of Scottish culture that dwells on dualities: where first readings deceive and things are not quite what they seem.

Jewellery is one area of Scottish contemporary craft that has achieved a relatively high degree of visibility. Exhibitions such as Hogg's twice curated *100%*

Proof – 'a distillation of new work in jewellery and silversmithing from Scotland'[8] – with venues in the United States of America and London, have led to international exposure. Ironically, these and other exhibitions have meant greater visibility outside Scotland for jewellery at least. Visibility within Scotland itself is another conundrum about Scottish crafts and is a major stumbling block to the general public's appreciation of its finest artist-makers. It is not only difficult to see work of emerging makers, but also well established figures. There is no dedicated venue for crafts, and few galleries in which contemporary applied arts have a starring role. Scotland has a strong cultural identity, but the applied arts suffer particularly from cliché and stereotype. The kitsch found in 'craft centres' the length and breadth of the country is very far from reality. Unless lucky enough to stumble upon the odd studio or workshop, public building, degree show, specialist boutique or gallery, or corner of a museum, the general public would be hard-pressed to find evidence of Scotland's 'cutting-edge' craftsmen or women.

The international commercial success of textile companies like Tait+Style or Timorous Beasties go some way to debunking the Scottish crafts stereotype. Tait+Style, based in the relatively remote Orkney Islands, creates witty versions of the ubiquitous tartan scarf and other typically Scottish accessory that sell in Tokyo and New York. Their work incorporates seaweed-like accretions, pom poms, Shetland knitting in jazzed-up colours and quirky appliqué, adapting industrial felting techniques for the fashion market. Glasgow-based design duo Timorous Beasties have recently produced printed textiles featuring scenes of sordid city park life, disguised in rustic terms in their 'Glasgow Toile', displaying their trademark style of elegantly presented, yet slightly disturbing, imagery. While not exhibiting in *The Cutting Edge*, these businesses demonstrate how humour and irony pervades some of the best of Scottish design and applied arts.

This is a theme explored by Laura Murray who makes 'wearable containers' from materials such as rope and ribbons, adorned with feathers or pom poms.

These are humorous takes on the sporran – a slightly comical aspect of Highland costume – playing with ideas on tradition and gender. It is amusing to conjure up an image of the self-respecting Scotsman wearing one of Murray's creations! Murray's background is jewellery and silversmithing, but her use of textile techniques and diverse materials, including recycled elements, is typical of the multi-media approach common in today's crafts.

When you think of Scottish textiles, a roll-call of classic brands instantly springs to mind: paisley, tartan, tweed, Shetland knitting, to name but a few. They are emblematic of Scotland's rich textile past, cultural and industrial heritage. International designers such as Vivienne Westwood and Comme des Garçons regularly appropriate such Scottish iconography, transforming it into avant-garde fashion. Similar deconstruction of tradition can be found in Jilli Blackwood's work. Her signature style – what she calls 'slash and show' – is a technique of applying layers of fabric, overlaid with embroidery and stitching that reveals the underlying cloth and frayed edges. Blackwood completely embellished the surface of a wool tartan kilt in her exuberant 2000 *Millennium Kilt* by layering bold jewel-like colours – turquoise, orange, crimson and acid green silks – in a kind of mimicry of the check weave. The resulting metamorphosis of this traditional garment is dynamic and outrageous.

Contemporary textiles is an extremely broad field, ranging from product design related primarily to interiors and furnishings, through ideas-based installations, to age-old techniques like knitting and weaving that are being constantly updated. Crossover elements between disciplines are also evident, as in Sara Keith and Roger Morris' collaborative work that explores metal techniques applied to textile structures. Considerable shifts in the scope of textiles have been made in the last ten years incorporating digital and other new technologies. Sarah Taylor was shortlisted for the Jerwood Applied Arts Prize in 2002 and her work with fibre optic technology within woven fabric is widely recognized as being at the forefront of experimental textiles. Normally tucked away in the sometimes isolated world of academia, it is a rare treat to experience Taylor's multi-sensory fabric installations, extraordinary creations that play with the reflective and light-emitting properties of optical fibres. In spite of the high-tech nature of her work, she aims to humanize these 'cutting-edge' technologies, expanding her ideas with new materials such as coloured paper yarns and coloured enamelled copper wire to create startlingly sensual and intriguing fabric forms.

The availability of resources such as Lottery-funding has led to a healthy rise in the number of architectural-related commissions in the last decade and a welcome strengthening of the place of the applied arts in complementing the built environment in both public and corporate spheres. While dogged by image and constructional problems, few can deny the drama of Edinburgh's new Scottish Parliament. A series of artworks were commissioned and purchased for various interior and external spaces about the building, that together form a fascinating essay on Scottish identity. These include superb commissions by two of Scotland's most highly respected textile artists. Both Maureen Hodge's tapestry and Norma Starszakowna's printed silk organza installation are rich in symbolic meaning, drawing on Scotland's eminent cultural history.

By contrast, but more typical of architectural commissions, is the Glasgow Homeopathic Hospital which features several integral art installations, including wall pieces by Jilli Blackwood and a series of woven willow forms by basket-maker, Lizzie Farey. However, in many ways the obvious specialist discipline for building-related art interventions is architectural glass, with its long and continuous association with stained-glass windows. Several exhibitors in *The Cutting Edge* have experience in this field, including Stephen Richard and Keiko Mukaide. Applied art installations are gradually becoming commonplace in Scotland's built environment and exemplify how specialist craft talent has found a new, imaginative and almost subliminal role in improving the quality of daily life.

Glass is a medium that is ripe with physical and metaphorical properties, and when allied with the skills needed to realize subtle ideas it can be extremely powerful. In parallel with international trends, Scottish glass is at a thrilling stage; whether architectural, conceptual, installation-based, or simply as exquisite objects, glass is a dynamic and expressive art form that readily explores the same areas as contemporary fine art. Edinburgh College of Art's Glass Department has become an international focus for students interested in experimenting in this medium, and North Lands Creative Glass in Lybster was established in the 1990s with the aim of stimulating interest in glass as an art form. With master classes, residencies and an annual conference, North Lands is widely regarded as an international centre of excellence. The pursuit of high standards of craftsmanship should not be taken for granted, however, and courses in materials-based disciplines are expensive to run. It is apparent that they are under increasing pressure within art colleges, already resulting in the closure of most ceramics departments in Scotland.

Alison Kinnaird's multi-disciplinary glass installations comprise copper-wheel engraving techniques alongside light effects from optical fibres and dichroic colour. Primarily concerned with depicting the human form, her finely modelled figures are set within scenes of activity, often within a symbolic framework. Kinnaird states in her website that her 'inspiration is firmly rooted in Scotland, though the references may not be literal or specific'.[9] These are subtle influences that yield a restrained colour palette, suggestive of a particular quality of light, inspired by air and water and recurring imagery. Likewise for Dorothy Hogg, the seascape of her home town in the west of Scotland is part of her artistic consciousness:

> Transient skies of every tone of grey with dark islands and headlands juxtaposed against a silvery changing sea. My eye is so attuned to these subtle and monochromatic tones that this has resulted in a tendency in my work to be restrained and understated.[10]

These references illustrate a decisive link between abstraction and landscape in Scottish visual art and the powerful presence of land and sea that is very evident in the crafts.

Keiko Mukaide's pursuit of understanding the nuances of place has become a kind of spiritual quest. Another Jerwood Prize candidate (1998), Mukaide has started to explore notions of geomancy to connect with 'earth energies', creating three-dimensional forms and site-specific glass sculptures and installations that make tangible somehow the 'spirit of place'. Scotland too has made its impact on Mukaide, originally from Tokyo. She talks of being 'inspired by the light of the north of Scotland which looked like dancing spotlights on the sea'.[11] Her new work involves the idea of a compass – a functional glass object to explore further the concept of 'location'.

The expression of nature and landscape takes many forms. Lizzie Farey departs from the functionality of traditional basket-making in her work, using willow and other local plants to create organic sculptural forms often described as 'nest-like tangles', a curious balance between order and chaos. And the economic and intense ideas in Sarah-Jane Selwood's ceramic pots seem to crystallize the notion of abstraction and landscape. Selwood's recent work develops the idea of slightly disturbing the perfection and simplicity of a thrown bowl by a series of precise cuts and inversions, creating a sense of spiralling movement that manipulates line, volume, shadow and form. Jeweller Ann Little's recent enamel work, simple forms with washed-out colours that echo land and sky, moss and lichen, depict the ever-changing qualities of light but with touches of decay as well. There is irony in making crumpled weathered-looking forms in enamel – something precious but distressed, resonant with the associations of discarded materials. This gives Little's work a kind of elegiac quality – a sense of paradise lost. Glimpses of an archetypal garden are to be found in Michael Lloyd's delicate chased silver and gold vessels, lyrical leaf and flower patterns rendered in a masterful command of technique. This 'homage to the natural world'[12] is typical of Lloyd's work, although recent copper vessels – what he calls 'weapons of peace', their forms suggestive of war – hint of trouble in paradise, reminiscent of the philosophical metaphors that abound in *Little Sparta*, Ian Hamilton Finlay's poetic garden.

Simon Ward's new home by the sea and frequent beach-combing have led him towards creating contemplative ceramic installations comprising vessels and porcelain 'tools' that are vaguely functional and incorporate driftwood and strangely sea-eroded found objects. The idea of containment – with its reference to box art form – invests these objects with further meaning. Grant McCaig similarly draws inspiration from the sea to create silver hollow vessels onto which he anchors trails of silver and bronze seaweed, shells and driftwood – forms that he describes as 'spaces for contemplation'. The landscape in its most literal sense has captured Rachel Hazell's imagination. A book artist who works in many different scales, Hazell's work includes large-scale sculptural book forms such as an ice-cliff made from paper and perspex, inspired by recent travels to Antarctica. For *The Cutting Edge* Hazell experiments with metal alongside more traditional book-binding, materials making reference to the landforms and jagged edges of the Scottish landscape.

The physical boundary and literal edges of land that have made such a powerful impact on the Scottish imagination seems a fitting place to end this perspective on Scottish crafts. Scotland's relatively small and, at times, hard to find first-rate crafts sector is culturally diverse and very much part of the international crafts community. While there are numerous common threads that draw these fragmentary voices together within this distinctive coastline, Scottish contemporary crafts are, nevertheless, a hybrid breed – strong in material traditions, elastic in definition, experimental and ground-breaking, and, above all, various. In the writer Robert Twigger's discussion about the threat of possible extinctions to our endangered planet, he states that 'the disappearance of diversity makes us just that bit less intelligent, flexible, human'.[13] There *is* a need for greater visibility for Scotland's finest applied artists, and exhibitions like *The Cutting Edge* are welcome indeed to set standards beyond the ordinary. Like Scotland's mythic fairy mountains, there is an underground seam yielding wonders to those who look hard enough. To conclude with Twigger again, it's 'that sense of delight that comes from being conscious of things being various'.[14]

ABOUT THE WRITER

Philippa Swann is a freelance writer based in Highland Perthshire who specializes in the applied arts. For ten years she contributed regularly to the Crafts Council's publication *Crafts*, as Contributing Editor for Scotland until August 2006. Previously she was Development Officer at the Edinburgh College of Art (1991-96), a position that introduced her to the extraordinary scope and excellence of practice in Scotland.

1 *20th-Century Scottish Poems*, selected by Douglas Dunn (Faber & Faber: London).
2 *The Millennium Collection for Bute House* (Incorporation of Goldsmiths of the City of Edinburgh).
3 'Sources of Inspiration', in *Crafts* Magazine, no. 157 (March/April 1999), p. 51.
4 Rosemary Hill, 'The 2001 Peter Dormer Lecture', in *Crafts* Magazine, no. 176 (May/June 2002), p. 46.
5 Martina Margetts, from 'A Daydream of Tiny Details', in *Crafts* Magazine, no. 155 (November/December 1998), p. 35.
6 *Crafts* Magazine, no. 191 (November/December 2004), p. 75.
7 *Dorothy Hogg 10 Year Retrospective 1994-2004*, with an introduction by Marina Vaizey (The Scottish Gallery).
8 *100% Proof* – A second generation of the distillation of new work in jewellery and silversmithing from Scotland (flow 2005).
9 www.alisonkinnaird.com
10 'Sources of Inspiration', in *Crafts* Magazine, no. 164 (May/June 2000), p. 51.
11 *Keiko Mukaide, Spirit of Place* catalogue (Talbot Rice Gallery: Edinburgh 2003).
12 *Michael Lloyd*, catalogue introduction by Amanda Game (The Scottish Gallery), 8 November to 1 December 2004.
13 Robert Twigger is the author of *The Extinction Club* (Penguin: London). This quotation was taken from *The Independent's* supplement, 'Disappearing World' (18 October 2005).
14 Robert Twigger, op. cit.

Artist
Malcolm Appleby

Born
1946, Beckenham, Kent,
England

Training
1961-68
Beckenham School of Art
Ravensbourne College of Art
    & Design
Central School of Arts & Crafts
Sir John Cass School of Art
Royal College of Art, London

Inspiration
Much of Malcolm Appleby's
inspiration comes from the
landscape and environment
surrounding his Perthshire
(and formerly Kincardine-
shire) home, and also from
many years of experimenting
with different methods and
techniques. Designs may be
expressionist or abstract,
figurative or decorative, and
draw on a wealth of inspiration – the natural world,
myths and elemental ideas,
and personal experience,
often revealing a mischievous
sense of humour.

Tools and processes
Engraving, carving, chasing,
hand raising, casting

Materials
Silver, gold, platinum, steel,
iron, bronze

**Examples of work in
public collections**
Aberdeen Art Gallery &
    Museums
National Museums Scotland,
    Edinburgh
Perth Museum and Art
    Gallery, Scotland
Victoria and Albert Museum,
    London

Statement
Malcolm Appleby is known
primarily as an engraver –
perhaps one of the most
original working in contemporary metal today. Malcolm
was introduced to engraving
at art school and then as a
part-time apprentice gun
engraver. These skills he later
applied to jewellery and metal
forms. Such an unconven-
tional background set the
pattern for his idiosyncratic
approach and style. Malcolm
describes creation of the art
object as the basis of his
working life:

'The simplest and least
expensive piece should have
the same inspirational quality
as my most valued major
works. Works of art should
be made for everyone to
enjoy. Engraving is central to
my design and art; it is from
engraving that my other skills
have evolved. I enjoy harnessing other craftsmen's skills
to extend my own creative
theories of form-related goldsmithing techniques.'

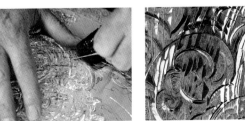

Artist Jilli Blackwood

Born
1965, Glasgow, Scotland

Training
1982-86 BA (Hons)
Embroidered and Woven
Textiles – The Glasgow
School of Art

Inspiration
'Inspiration is a magical process. The connection for it is
only understood by the artist.'

Tools and processes
'Slash and show' process;
scissors, needles, sewing
machine and dyes

Materials
All natural fibres, silks,
cottons, linens

**Examples of work in
public collections**
Aberdeen Asset Management
plc
Glasgow Museums and Art
Galleries
National Museums Scotland,
Edinburgh
United States Consulate,
Edinburgh

Statement
'I created my "slash and
show" technique whilst a
student at Glasgow School of
Art and I have been refining
and developing it since.
'I combine texture, colour
and design as the three
elements that provide my
alchemy. Different textiles
take dye differently, cut and
fray differently, and absorb
light differently. I like to combine these uncertain factors
in my work as a foil to the
discipline and rigidity of
formal design. The clash of
the two creates both tension
and a sense of serenity.
'A textile is expected to
behave in a certain way,
to be laid across a bed, to
clothe and protect from the
elements, or to flutter in the
sky proclaiming a Nation's
existence. My fabrics are
there to be looked at in contrast to their surroundings,
and to challenge the viewer
to re-think their perceptions
of the function of fabric.
'The very nature of my
work, in which leather, natural silks, wools and cottons
are hand dyed, sewn together
in layers and hand cut, defies
the precision of modern
design, not detracting from it
but complementing it.'

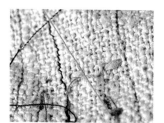

Artist
Ruth Chalmers

Born
1980, Dundee, Scotland

Training
1998-2002 Duncan of
    Jordanstone College of Art
    and Design, University of
    Dundee

Inspiration
'My work is all based around
the ideas of movement and
childhood games, family life
and domestic rituals – I love
the kitsch and comedic. The
idea of plan and fun is always
foremost.'

Tools and processes
Silver solder techniques,
enamelling, wire work using
a variety of pliers and snips
and stakes; also collage-type
techniques

Materials
Silver wire and sheet,
enamels, found objects
including wood

Statement
'Based on images of domestic
rituals, family life and comical
antics of animals, I strive to
create pieces that are playful
and humorous; and whether
making small-scale jewellery
or large-scale sculptural
pieces, I like to add a movable
element to them.
    'I also love playing around
with different types of
materials and using unusual
or new techniques or blends
that I haven't tried before.

To me, it's not about how
much the materials cost that
makes a piece precious, rather
the image process and the
reaction that counts.
    'I never want my work to
be intimidating to anyone; I
make it because I enjoy it and
want others simply to enjoy it
too. You can interpret the
pieces as you wish – some
may find the pieces evocative
of childhood memories, as a
lot of the images come from
childhood for instance. Some
pieces do have a story behind
them – but I don't want that
to be a requirement to enjoy-
ing them. I don't want people
to think they need to get too
bogged down in that!'

Artist
Peter Chang

Born
1944, London, England

Training
1968-71 Postgraduate
Diploma in Printmaking
and Sculpture – The Slade
School of Fine Art,
University College, London
1966-67 Postgraduate in
Sculpture – Liverpool
College of Art, Liverpool.
Printmaking at Atelier 17,
Paris, France
1963-66 Diploma in Art and
Design in Graphic Design –
Liverpool College of Art

1962-63 Foundation –
Liverpool College of Art

Inspiration
Nature/man-made objects

Tools and processes
Many

Materials
Acrylic, resin, silver and gold

**Examples of work in
public collections**
Victoria and Albert Museum,
London
Museum of Art and Design,
New York, USA
Powerhouse Museum,
Sydney, Australia
Schmuck Museum, Pforzheim,
Germany

Statement
'People often comment on
the fact that I work with a
material which they consider

in itself to be worthless.
Diamonds, marble, gold,
canvas and paint, as materials,
are nothing in themselves
until their creative potential
is explored, exposed and
fused through vision, intellect,
instinct and the hands of
artists, sculptors and craftsmen.
'The same is true of plastics.
It is the magical potential of
materials that I find fascinating. Plastics in their own
right have little intrinsic value.
It is the joy of exploring their
qualities of malleability,
creating colour and sensuality,
teasing the materials to obey,
exploiting all to the maximum,
which gives it value to me, to
previous practitioners, and
to the increasing number of
artists and craftsmen who
love to create through it.'

Artist
Gillian Cooper

Born
1970, Motherwell, Scotland

Training
2001-05 Goldsmiths College,
London

Inspiration
How to protect children in
a city; surveillance and CCTV
cameras

Tools and processes
Digital knitting machine and
felting

Materials
Wool, cotton, acrylic and
lurex

Statement
'These pieces are the culmination of two years of work
spent exploring the concepts
of protection and surveillance.
   'Protecting children in
today's society is a difficult
balance between giving them
the freedom to develop and
shielding them for their own
good. We are constantly
filmed on CCTV in our cities,
but does it only record or
actually prevent dreadful
happenings? Is the man
protecting or abducting
the child? By creating these
images in knit, it gives them
a blanket-like quality,
emphasizing protection
and warmth.
   'My key stimuli are colour,
architecture, unusual natural
forms and texture. How a
piece feels is important to
me, which is why I work in
textiles as I can control and
vary the surface impact.
   'I enjoy using traditional
textile techniques in unusual
or contemporary ways. This
can be knit, as here, or by
making large scale 3-D patch-
work shelters.
   'Having just moved to a
rural location after 15 years
of living in major cities, my
work is beginning to change
as I am constantly inspired by
my surroundings.'

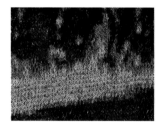

Artist
Jack Cunningham

Born 1953, Glasgow

Training
2001 to date PhD (P/T) –
    Glasgow School of Art
1988-89 Teaching certificate
    – Jordanhill College of
    Education
1972-76 Duncan of Jordan-
    stone College of Art and
    Design, Univ. of Dundee
1971-72 Glasgow College of
    Building (Interior Design)

Inspiration
'What really excites me are the
ordinary things I see in everyday life. No matter where I
am, images of the obscure
and unexpected become
source material that stimulate
and underpin my subsequent
design development.'

Tools and processes
'My brooches are generally
fabricated. The equipment
and technical processes are
linked to my creative process
and how best to realize the
narrative of each piece. My
work is not defined through
the utilisation of a particular
tool, technique or material.'

Materials
'Materials range from an
eclectic mix of the precious
and non-precious – metal,
gemstones, pearls, found
objects or "ready-mades".'

**Examples of work in
public collections**
Crafts Council, London
Museum of Decorative Arts,
    Montreal, Canada
National Museums Scotland,
    Edinburgh
Princeton University Chapel

Statement
'I work exclusively with the
brooch form to explore
personal narrative themes. I
am interested in the construct
of our relationships with
family, people and place, with
recollection and memory, how
we engage with life and face
death. I mostly experience
this through travel, having
made numerous visits to
Japan, and through time
spent between homes in
Glasgow and Paris.
    'Narrative jewellery is
a powerful means of com-
munication and tells us something of the designer-maker.
It indicates a conscious statement by the wearer, who
then becomes the vehicle
through which a wider
audience views the work.
For the wearer, there exists
the potential to re-interpret
the work according to their
personal frame of reference.
A triangular relationship is
formed, between *maker-
wearer-viewer*.

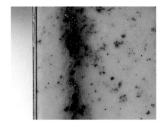

Artist
Stooshie Design
Linda Carlin and Archie
Manson

Born
Linda
1956, Ayrshire, Scotland
Archie
1964, Ayrshire, Scotland

Training
Linda
1992-96 Jewellery and
    Silversmithing – The
    Glasgow School of Art
Archie
1984-88 BSc Architecture –
    University of Strathclyde,
    Glasgow

Inspiration
'Our most recent work
involves one-off large art
panels inspired by a variety
of sources which includes
science, nature, abstraction
and dream narrative. Everyday work concentrates on
batch production of contemporary acrylic key rings.'

Tools and processes
'A variety of hand and
electric saws, a lathe and
laser cutting are utilized to
layer, slice and turn new
colours and striped pieces
from acrylic sheet.'

Materials
Acrylic sheet

Statement
'Producing original, contemporary pieces and experi-
mentation with materials has
been the main driving force

behind the Stooshie partnership from the beginning.
  'Originally working in
wood and metal, a move into
acrylics was made in 2004 to
allow a more contemporary
edge to develop; colour
experimentation has resulted
in the production of muted
shades not normally associated with this material.
  'While most of our output
has a clearly understood and
almost ethereal quality, the
occasional vibrant piece
sneaks under the wire incorporating vivid reds, oranges,
limes, yellows, turquoise, etc,
usually in response to a minimal interior setting in need
of a dynamic focal point.
  'Working with such a flat,
unyielding material is a
challenge and can often be a
frustrating process, but the
final pieces we feel are
worth the effort.'

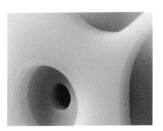

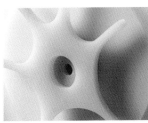

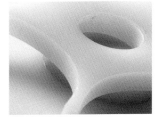

Artist
Mark Devlin

Born
1967, Musselburgh, Scotland

Training
1990-94   BA Hons 3-D Design
– University of Central
Lancashire

Inspiration
Scandinavian, Shaker and
Japanese design style

Tools and processes
Vacuum bag press laminating
birch ply

Materials
Wood, metal and glass:
birch, beech, oak, aluminium
and steel

Statement
'I have always been, and
continue to be, influenced by
Scandinavian design and the
Shaker movement. These two
quite distinct design styles
have had within them the
potential to create artefacts,
which are at once functional
and minimal on the one
hand, yet subtle and very
beautiful on the other.
Pursuit of this ideal has been
key to the development and
ethos of my design identity.

'Like a lot of Scandinavian
furniture, my designs have
been formed using lamin-
ating processes – layers of
wood are glued together
and held over formers under
considerable pressure. This
process demands its proper
discipline and integrity, but
rewards you with clear
structural coherence of form
in the finished piece. Also
like these two movements,
my work is designed primarily
with use in mind – most of
the pieces fold and stack.

'Recently I have been
experimenting with a vacuum
bag press to do the laminating process. This relatively
new technology allows me
to produce new designs
which are a lot more com-
plex, yet quicker and easier
to produce. I also have plans
to experiment in using the
press to mould thin sheets
of metal. This is still very
much in the early stages of
development, but it would
potentially open up all sorts
of creative possibilities.'

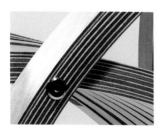

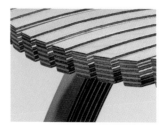

Artist
Lizzie Farey

Born 1962, Singapore

Training
1980-81 Cardiff College of
    Art
1979-80 Canterbury College
    of Art

Inspiration
'Galloway: the hills and lochs
and wild materials that grow
there.'

Tools and processes
Secateurs, bodkin, sharp
knife, weaving and
interlacing

Materials
Willow, ash, larch, heather
and birch

**Examples of work in
public collections**
The City of Edinburgh
    Museums & Galleries
National Museums Scotland,
    Edinburgh
The Shipley Art Gallery,
    Gateshead

Statement
'I have a fascination with
living things and natural
form. I find an exhilarating
freedom in the opportunity
to explore undiscovered
forms and a new relation to
nature.

'My local area, Galloway,
is the rich source of my
inspiration, not only for the
landscape of hills and lochs,
heather and larch, but also
for the many varieties
of willow that I can grow
and harvest in nearby fields.
The withies, with their freight
of pussy willows soft as a
spaniel's ear, range in colour
from ochre through maroon
and chestnut to nearly black,
and have the soft lustre of
oiled wood. The work is
sensual, contemplative and
slightly mysterious: often,
despite the open weave, you
cannot see to the centre.

'I love to work randomly,
allowing the materials to
reveal themselves. I work
with a simple form in mind,
mostly a globe, open bowl or
ring. There is a process that
you have to go through
which is chaos, and absolute
concentration and an
enduring belief is necessary
before order and stillness can
return.

'Starting out as a tradi-
tional basket-maker some 15
years ago, willow has become
for me a medium for an
interaction with nature that
is deeply personal.'

Artist Ray Flavell

Born 1944, Bilston, England

Training
2001 Doctor of Philosophy – Edinburgh College of Art
1972 Orrefors Glass School Sweden
1965 Postgraduate Diploma Product Design – Wolverhampton College of Art
1964 National Diploma in Design – Wolverhampton College of Art

Inspiration
'Glass is a wonderful material endowed with so many special qualities. Working with glass as a hot viscous fluid or as a cold hard brittle material allows me to interpret ideas literally from nature and to reflect upon contemporary concepts for inspiration.'

Tools and processes
'The work is made at the furnace by blowing and forming techniques; also some pieces are constructed using a combination of flat glass and blown forms bonded together. Cold working techniques are also used, including sawing, cutting, polishing and sandblasting.

Materials Glass

Examples of work in public collections
Crafts Council Collection, London
National Museums Scotland, Edinburgh
Victoria and Albert Museum, London
National Museum of Art, Tokyo

Statement
'I work with traditional techniques and hope to express my own view of the world grounded in these. I use craft to make art, so glass becomes a medium of artistic expression. Glass-blowing and cutting, polishing and various other surface treatments provide ample means to allow me to express my ideas using vessel forms – a long-standing device of civilization.

'I work with the notion that transparency, through the section of glass, suggests the medium in which life exists and evolves. The sea, atmosphere, even the electronic world of cyberspace, have inspired much of my work.

'Currently I am looking at conventional glass artefacts (bowls, phials, window glass) to express a state of mind or temperament. When these objects are distorted and presented in a different context, they take on a new meaning and can become metaphors for us. I aim to do this through the glassiness of glass.'

A RIGHTFUL PLACE IN THE SCHEME OF THINGS: A HISTORY OF CRAFT RESOURCES IN SCOTLAND

Simon Olding

In 1981, as a young Assistant Keeper in the Decorative Arts Department of Glasgow Museums and Art Galleries, I was given the enviable task of helping to organize an exhibition by the mercurial artist Alexander Leckie[1] by Brian Blench, the Keeper of the Department since its foundation in 1973. It was my first sustained exposure to contemporary craft, and I can still recall the drama and passion of the run-up to the exhibition, as well as the prodigious amount of wine served at the private view. Alex, diminutive in size, expansive in personality, had worked ferociously hard to produce a notable body of work. It varied from conventional stoneware vessels through to 'Fungi landscapes', dark and introspective bronze bandaged heads from a 1968 series 'Images of War', with a central feature of rather jaunty erotic pots. It was a bravura exhibition.

Harry Jefferson Barnes, sometime Director of The Glasgow School of Art,[2] wrote a perceptive essay on Leckie's life and career for the catalogue, concluding:

> I am most grateful to Glasgow Museums and Art Galleries for creating for Alex this opportunity and responsibility to show Glasgow his measure as an artist, which is what he came home to do. It is part of their vigorous new policy to give the so-called applied arts their rightful place in the scheme of things.
>
> It is sad that it is the closing exhibition of the St Enoch Exhibition Centre which brought so many good things right into the commercial centre of Glasgow. One hopes that it will be adequately replaced.[3]

A number of issues, pertinent to this essay, are wrapped up in this statement. The whole edifice is supported, of course, by the individual maker: on this occasion the much travelled Leckie, returning romantically to his Glasgow home. But the structure supporting the craft exhibition is vital for its success: the public funds; the public venue. And a policy framework also lies beneath the event, as well as the considerations of the small band of decision-makers with a professional responsibility for the crafts. It was a fragile balancing act then, and it is a fragile balancing act now.

The interplay of maker, venue, private and public ambition (and private/public sales), of aesthetic and financial values, is a constant feature of the crafts sector across the United Kingdom. There are particular shifts that have a particular Scottish dimension, and this essay endeavours to point some of them out. Barnes hinted at the fluidity of craft developments: a policy that looked to be in limbo; a venue that was facing closure. It is certainly true that craft initiatives in Scotland since, say, the pivotal period from 1990 onwards, have veered from the exceptional to the transient. Success as well as failure has marked Scottish contemporary craft activity.

But the successes have often been transformational, the experiments bold. Very little regret marks the failed ventures, although a number of Scottish commentators bemoan the fact that the crafts in Scotland are promoted apologetically, rather than with vigour and passion. The crafts in Scotland have, since the 1950s, developed in a 'commercial' model rather than an aesthetic one. State support has mostly been tempered by the approach to sustain a business first and worry about the contribution to cultural activity as a second best. The economic factor has been inevitable because the funding has often derived from a governmental economic development arm, and even later state funding directly through the cultural arm of state has carried the money message. As Victor Margie commented: 'The greatest difference between Scotland and [the Crafts Advisory Committee] is that Scotland places greater emphasis on employment and craft industries rather than on the individual craftsman.'[4] The St Enoch Exhibition Centre was leased to the Museums Department by the Scottish Development Agency,[5] which had assumed arm's length responsibility for crafts development via its crafts division until 1991.

Indeed, when the first Scottish Craft Centre was established in Edinburgh in 1949, its founding grant came from the Scottish Committee of the Council of

Industrial Design.[6] This committee established 'priorities for the development of crafts and home industries, an aspect of their remit which was gradually demitted to the fledgling Scottish Craft Centre'.[7] The Scottish Craft Centre was the first organisation to promote and sell contemporary craft. It laid a path for other national developments: the gathering of a dispersed and discrete collection of modern and contemporary crafts throughout key Scottish museums, for example. Its range was broad: from traditional, often rurally-based craft work (textile lengths, sporrans), through to contemporary tapestry and silver. But, rather like the Crafts Council in England (but with a more distinguished architectural history), the venue was in a heritage building not a contemporary one. This was due, it has to be said, to the impressive philanthropy of the Bute family who restored the 1630s Canongate town house which served as the headquarters of the Centre until its demise in 1991. This demise can be characterized with brevity as a victim of the tensions between traditionalists and craft innovators.

Proposals in 1991 for a successor body to the Scottish Craft Centre – a Scottish Crafts Council bearing a resemblance to the UK-wide, but London-based, Crafts Council – were loudly heard. Earlier plans 'to pass responsibility for the crafts to the Scottish Arts Council were abandoned'.[8] This was a pivotal time for craft politics and developments across the UK, especially important north of the border since the infrastructure was so vulnerable. Government support for the crafts in Scotland was removed from the Crafts Division of the Scottish Development Agency, and a proposal made to replace it with a new marketing and commercial service called Scotland by Design; a title no doubt deliberately chosen to announce a new era, and to forgo the specific association with craft.

This institutional turmoil went down badly with SALVO, the Scottish Arts Lobby, much as the proposal by Richard Wilding in 1989 unilaterally to remove the independent status of the Crafts Council and merge it within the Arts Council was seen as hostile by many in the crafts constituency in England.[9] But the

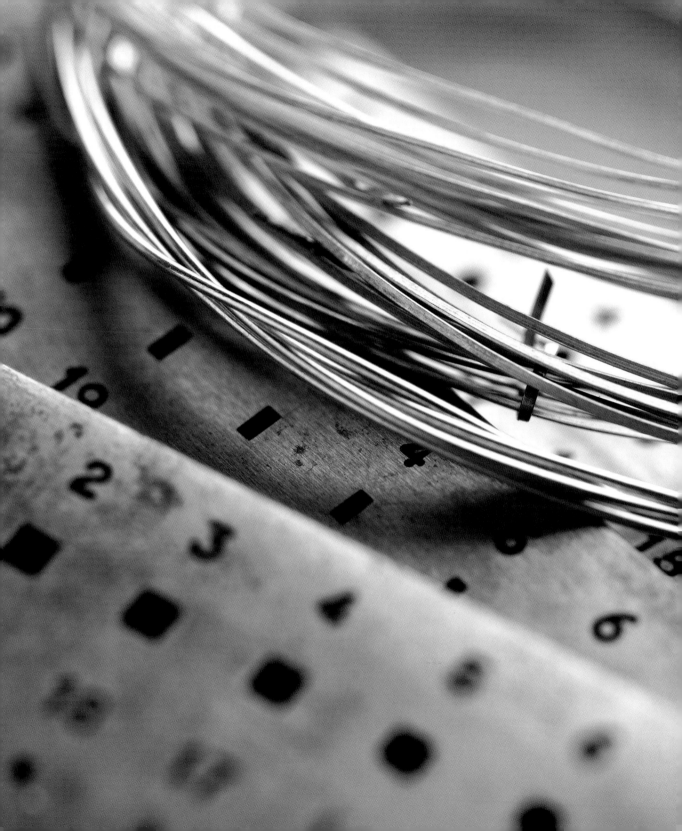

proposed focus on a commercial imperative had a track record, if a modest one, behind it. Civil servants could see that small craft businesses contributed (primarily, as it were) to tourism and economic welfare. The new agency was designed to provide business and training advice and, pragmatically, to organize trade fairs. Matters of strategic support for the education infrastructure and the development of creative practice were not seen as a priority for policy-making. The plans for Scotland by Design were driven by sales. The Minister of Industry and Local Government (no culture ministry here) gave a strict time limit to this offer. Scotland by Design had to be profitable within five years. SALVO was withering in its commentary, finding the proposals 'ill-informed, insensitive and retrograde … the evidence we have is that [the proposal] has shocked and angered the crafts community. Indeed, compared with their English colleagues, they see themselves as second-class citizens, less well-off than before.'[10]

Scotland has always handled radical protest with verve. At around the same time as SALVO was digging in its critical heels, Action for Applied Arts was formed (in 1992): a direct consequence of the closure of the crafts division. Its purpose was 'to lobby Government for support for the crafts'.[11] The new group provided a lobbying forum for its members, but it also had creative ambitions, to provide 'excellence and innovation in the crafts'. This was achieved through well-managed selling exhibitions such as *Value Added* at Aberdeen Art Gallery and the acclaimed *Tented House of the Arts* at the 1992 Edinburgh International Festival. Today the retitled Applied Arts Scotland (Chair, Rosemary Watt) continues the work of directing continuing professional development opportunities to makers, as well as disseminating information to its supporters.

By 1993 a policy settlement was reached, and the decision to transfer support for the crafts to the Scottish Arts Council was finally enacted. The Secretary of State for Scotland allocated £300,000 of funds for this express purpose. The decision brought together, for the first time, the voice of the cultural planner, the maker, the educationalist, and the public and commercial aspects of the crafts together under one roof. The crafts could be seen as an agent of economic and cultural change. The first advisory committee for crafts under the auspices of the Scottish Arts Council was chaired not by an economist, but by an academic and practising jeweller with an international reputation: Professor Eric Spiller from The Robert Gordon University. Dr Helen Bennett, sometime Crafts Officer at the Scottish Development Agency, took over as the founder Head of Crafts at the Scottish Arts Council. Consistency, policy stability, and modest levels of enhanced funding to lead strategic developments for the crafts by the state, have been the positive outcomes of this landmark policy decision.[12]

Craft policy in England has not been so settled during this period, and the turbulence of the Wilding review has not yet been seen through to a stable end point. The announcement of a new document, a *Draft National Strategy for Crafts* (Arts Council England 2005) noted, optimistically, that 'Arts Council England provides leadership for the crafts in England with our partners including the Crafts Council'. The fact that the paper was not offered for full open consultation with these 'partners', and that the successor *Draft National Action Plan* (February 2006) is manifestly a policy paper for Arts Council England itself, rather than the whole craft community, demonstrates a rather more timorous approach to policy. The major strategic review of the Crafts Council in 2005 and 2006 has also been (to the chorus of criticism from many makers and craft historians) an internalized affair, although it is far too early to tell if the changes that are proposed (the Crafts Council will become a purely 'strategic body' delivering activity through other organisations) will have lasting effect. There was, certainly, none of the forthright and open consultation that marked the Scottish Arts Council's inheritance of direct responsibility for the crafts in Scotland. These are telling differences.

Certainly, the Scottish Arts Council demonstrated early pride in its leadership for the crafts. This pride was also matched by a visible statement of intent to focus resources directly to craft practitioners. In December 1994 the Council

had unveiled commissions in its new reception area by 'some of its leading crafts-people', after a national competition. The outcome was furniture designed by Kenneth Anderson and made by John Souter, as well as a wall hanging by Norma Starszakowna, together with a large rug woven by the acclaimed Edinburgh Tapestry Company.[13]

In the Scottish Arts Council's report *Building Bridges*,[14] the policy objectives for state funding for the crafts were presented: 'To create opportunities to encourage people to experience and understand contemporary crafts, and to help craftspeople make, promote and sell their output and enhance their skills.' It was a modest but deliverable objective. The economic value of the crafts is linked, explicitly now, to a wider access agenda, and the sense of a fruitful engagement with the public, despite the didactic ring to the word 'understand' (and the lack of a place for, say, enjoyment and celebration). But it was the start of a new holistic approach to craft policy and, as such, was visionary. One counterpart in England is worth noting: the exemplary report *The real world*[15] undertaken by South West Arts (led by the Crafts Officer Erica Steer) in its final guise as a regional arts board. This report still stands as a model of good practice for evidence-led policy, backed up by commentary from makers and craft players.

The Scottish Arts Council's document was unashamedly an advocacy report, a picture book. It also celebrated the notable achievements of the Crafts Department and, as Christine Rew notes, 'effectively demonstrated that financial investment led to tangible results in a strengthened crafts sector in Scotland'.[16] In passing, the report also highlighted the need, still pressing, for an authoritative history of the crafts in Scotland, post 1950. Scotland's craft writing has had something of a chequered history. The journal *Craftwork: Scotland's Craft magazine* (funded by the Scottish Craft Centre, the Highlands and Islands Development Board and the Small Industries Council for Rural Areas of Scotland) ran from 1972 to 1988.[17] Coverage from this point was handled within the Crafts Council's *Crafts*. Philippa Swann was appointed the role of the contributing editor for Scotland in 1999, replacing Paul Nesbitt. There is undoubtedly a major book, still to be written, on modern and contemporary crafts in Scotland.

State support for the crafts has been one demonstrable factor in the continuing success of the sector, built, inevitably, on a thousand decisions by individual makers to forge creative careers. This support has been maintained within reasonable limits. It has been matched by independent activity within the private and commercial sectors, by initiatives driven from the Scottish art schools and universities, and by specific maker-led projects. These developments also give texture and value to the creativity of the crafts in Scotland. Quality is sometimes more of an issue than quantity. Scotland is not, for example, abundantly served by specialist, independent craft galleries. The Independent Crafts Galleries Association only covers England and Wales, and names 24 participating galleries there. A survey by the Crafts Council in 1999 listed only seven specialist shops in Scotland, compared to say 15 in the South East of England. But this gives a partial picture. There is a current flourishing network of open studio events, such as 'Spring Fling' in Dumfries and Galloway, and the sustained quality of the key private sector galleries has been impressive. The mantle has fallen on the few, it is true, but in venues such as The Scottish Gallery in Edinburgh and the Roger Billcliffe Gallery, Glasgow, discernment and a close watch on emerging as well as established makers are positive contributions to the crafts narrative in Scotland.

The presentation of crafts started at the Roger Billcliffe Gallery in 1992 when Margie Roberts organized a small jewellery exhibition. The policy took hold from 1994 onwards, when Lynn Park, herself a Glasgow School of Art trained graduate, focussed exhibitions in jewellery, ceramics, metalwork, furniture, glass and wood.[18] A selection held a mirror, to some degree, up to the high reputation and the products of the Scottish art schools, particularly in the fields of metalwork and jewellery. Jack Cunningham and Graham Stewart were two internationally acclaimed practitioners who exhibited and sold regularly through the gallery. Quality has been Parks' watchword, along with a desire for innovative work, demonstrating consummate hand-skill. Her later selection of makers, such as Sarah Hutchison and Georgia Wiseman, were balanced by the need to wait patiently for a period after graduation (sometimes up to five years) to assess if preferred makers had 'staying power' and the ability 'to stretch the line' of innovative design and use of materials.[19]

Amanda Game's role at The Scottish Gallery has been similarly influential. The gallery is the senior exhibitor of contemporary crafts in Scotland. The private sector has showed Scottish contemporary craft with far more regularity than the museum sector, to the credit of the former, and The Scottish Gallery is the pioneer. Game herself has had some 20 years' experience there of assembling high quality contemporary craft for sale, seeking out and nurturing new talent, whether local or international.[20] She takes a robust view of the major craft retail activity in Scotland. She views the commercial gallery network as the best place for high quality (and necessarily modest-scale) as well as often high value items. A stable portfolio of named makers of established reputation forms the backbone of the presenting artists. The larger-scale (and often riskier, as well as more traditional) craft fairs need different motivations and characteristics if they are to succeed in Scotland as anything other than a redoubtable 'trade' fair or a paler version of Chelsea Crafts Fair.

There has been a turbulent history here. Both Dazzle (regularly) and the Craft Movement (occasionally) have shown in Scotland. Artisan, at first subtitled 'The Edinburgh Festival of Contemporary Crafts',[21] was established in the hope that it would remain a prestigious and long-lived selling exhibition for the crafts. The Festival directors stated:

> Our aim is for Artisan to flourish for a long time yet, becoming an annual fixture here at Festival time. There is potential ... for increasing the number of exhibitors and the scope of the whole event.[22]

It launched ambitiously at the Edinburgh International Festival in 1997, coinciding with the Festival's 50th anniversary, with 135 makers, but only lasted for two more seasons, eventually closing in 2002.[23] Game puts this down less to hubris (Artisan was reported to be 'the largest crafts festival in Europe', a strapline echoed by the Chelsea Crafts Fair 25th anniversary headline 'Europe's Finest Crafts Fair') than to a lack of national distinctiveness. It was a Chelsea model, right for Chelsea, but launched on Edinburgh perhaps without sufficient grounding, or marketing presence, and therefore not giving enough of the chance to develop an audience and cultivate collector's support over the longer term. The investment by the Scottish Arts Council in Artisan can be read as a questionable decision, but it may be more appropriate to praise the funding as a notable effort in an environment that called for risk-taking.

If the Artisan model of starting large and lasting briefly offered one means of distributing and presenting Scottish contemporary crafts, then the 'organic' growth of the North Lands Creative Glass in Caithness offers an alternative exemplar. North Lands demonstrates, better than many other cultural organisations, the consequence of an enlightened, practitioner-led development, nurtured by public and private funds, small in setting, but inventive in scope, and quickly setting an international standard. Modelled on the renowned Pilchuck Glass School in America, North Lands was set up through the pioneering vision of Dan Klein and Robert Maclennan MP, with Tessa Clegg as the founder artistic director.

Financial support from the Scottish Arts Council and the Jerwood Foundation was instrumental, helping to set North Lands on its way as an education-led craft workshop and conference. Ten years later, North Lands celebrated with a major exhibition at the National Museum of Scotland and The Scottish Gallery in 2006. It has, as Edmund de Waal observed, redrawn 'boundaries between glass artists, performance and sculpture. Unaffiliated to institutions, it has all the brio and energy consequent on discovering a synergy between unlikely artists'.[24] Now that the Edinburgh College of Art runs the sole surviving glass course in Scotland (and The Glasgow School of Art the last ceramics course), the longevity and the creative spirit of North Lands is perhaps needed in Scotland more than ever before.[25]

The debt to the Scottish art schools[26] should not be underestimated, however. It is still significant, even if the areas of taught craft practice are narrowing. The international reputations of maker-educators such as Dorothy Hogg (Edinburgh College of Art) and Jack Cunningham (The Glasgow School of Art) have drawn in young practitioners, as well as research and development resources. The crafts sector needs its stars in academic institutions as well as in the studio. The public sector has also provided the means to support craft commissioning throughout Scotland, for public buildings and spaces. There is an increasingly specialist 'collection' of these works (which are permanent and temporary in nature) in the built and natural environments (and perhaps there is another book to be written about craft outside the museum walls in Scotland). One of the most evocative and pivotal commissions has proved to be Tim Stead's robust furniture for the Café Gandolfi, Glasgow, one of a powerful series of his works in the public domain across Scotland.[27]

The Scottish Arts Council has been a major force in promoting commissioning, leading, as we have seen, by example. Large-scale development projects, often facilitated by Art in Partnership, set up in 1985 as the first public art agency in Scotland, often came with the resources to add keynote craft commissions. Notable examples include Elizabeth McFall's mosaic pavements in Arbroath,[28] or her ceramic tile design for the rotunda of the then new Scottish Office building in Leith.[29] Signature public buildings, such as Glasgow's Gallery of Modern Art, the High Court of Justiciary, Glasgow, the Sheriff Court House and High Court in Edinburgh, all revelled in imaginative placements and integrated schemes, working with Scottish makers and English practitioners such as Gary Breeze, Sasha Ward and Matthew Burt, whose furniture (made in Wiltshire) was placed at An Tuireann, the Arts Centre on the Isle of Skye, between 1998 and 2002.[30]

Keiko Mukaide has built up a formidable reputation for her elegant, precise and often gracefully reticent glassworks in the public domain in Scotland: for example, at the Hub in Edinburgh, and in 2000 at the Royal Botanic Gardens Edinburgh. Something of a culmination of this approach to setting craft work in public space has been reached (a comma rather than a full stop, it is to be hoped) with the commissioning programme for the new Scottish Parliament building, project-managed by Art in Partnership. The works, according to Philippa Swann, gathered in leading contemporary Scottish[31] artists and charted 'a fascinating essay on Scottish identity with an emphasis on the land'. Major pieces by renowned makers such as Alison Kinnaird and Maureen Hodge highlighted 'profound expressions of what it means to be Scottish'.[32]

The energy behind placing large-scale commissions is not a purely Scottish phenomenon, although the attempt, in key locations (and no more so than in the Scottish Parliament), to give visual and tactile significance to the theme of national identity, is more common than in England. Scotland has always been open to UK-wide competitions. Similarly, Scottish museum collections of modern and contemporary crafts are, in essence, UK collections, with Scottish components playing a major role. There is no stand-alone museum collection of modern craft (and no stand-alone museum of Scottish contemporary crafts) in Scotland. The Scottish crafts sector is not fundamentally building-based. The collections are, in truth, less visible than they merit, and it is significant that when the Crafts Gallery opened at the then Royal Museum, Edinburgh as late as in 1998, it was billed as 'the first national centre for contemporary crafts in Scotland' (although this was perhaps harsh on the by then long closed Scottish Craft Centre).[33]

This lack of a signature and large-scale museum space for the crafts has proved a weakness as well as strength. There is no institutional jealousy; but there is no co-ordinated, large-scale touring for the crafts. There is a distributed, flexible, system, not a structure defined by buildings. The vision of the then Glasgow Museums Director, Trevor Walden, in establishing the first specialist

Decorative Arts Department in Scotland (it ran from 1973 to 2002) gave a major boost to collecting contemporary crafts throughout the country.[34] There are major collections (one thinks of the unheralded but highly impressive Scottish pottery collections at Paisley, for example, and the world class jewellery collections at National Museums Scotland), but they do not always force their way aggressively into the museum landscape. These collections are also, naturally enough, located in the key urban centres, and have been led in the main by national and local authority initiatives (at Glasgow, Edinburgh, Aberdeen, Paisley and Dundee).[35] A much-needed spark to craft collecting was brought about by the National Collecting Scheme for Scotland, promoted by the Contemporary Art Society. The first phase, involving the Aberdeen and Dundee museums, had a catalytic effect on their collections, both in terms of adding substantive new work, and in raising the confidence levels of the curatorial teams expressed in the purchase of innovative works of contemporary craft.

There has been some imaginative transferring of collections in the public domain. For example, the craft collection established, without precedence, by the Scottish Development Agency, was gifted to National Museums Scotland on the Agency's demise. The collection had been brought together first by the Scottish Craft Centre (and called the Scottish Crafts Collection) and was shown in various exhibitions in destinations as varied as the Pier Arts Centre, Stromness, and in Piccadilly's in the Strand, London.

But the provision is less well off than in England, where there have been a number of highly significant new museum and gallery developments in the crafts in recent years. The Hub, Sleaford, the new galleries at Hove and Brighton Museums, the Craft and Design Galleries at Manchester and the establishment of the Crafts Study Centre (still the first and only UK museum designed and built for a modern craft collection), all provoke an interest in why Scotland's museums have not created discrete space for its crafts. There is nothing to match the expectation, for example, of the new Middlesborough Institute of Modern Art

(MIMA) and The Lightbox in Woking in 2007, as new buildings which create major space for craft collections and exhibitions. Perhaps a national museum for the crafts in Scotland would act as a vital rallying place for contemporary crafts, stamping an authoritative character and giving much-needed space for the rich and mainly hidden public collection of crafts.

The picture of exhibiting the crafts in Scottish museums and galleries is also patchy. There have been impressive exceptions, to be sure, but the space given to contemporary craft exhibitions is relatively limited, and a modest number of key venues shares the load, often led by a small but highly experienced band of dedicated curators, such as Christine Rew at Aberdeen and Laura Hamilton at the enterprising Collins Gallery, University of Strathclyde, in Glasgow.[36] Scotland's independent initiatives in the crafts are also a feature of the landscape. Most recently, a new ad hoc group has been set up, with the title 'Innovative Craft', to provide opportunities for a new sequence of independently curated craft exhibitions, with a flexible, institution-less agenda – a version of the North Lands model, but on tour.

The strategic decisions taken by the Scottish Arts Council have done much to sustain the vulnerable crafts sector. Working pragmatically (that is, within the limits of officer time and relatively modest budgets), the Scottish Arts Council has, impressively, used consultative approaches to underpin shifts in resources, so that a small number of key organisations can have space to develop and thrive. This has been especially true of North Lands, the investment in the network of craft development officers throughout Scotland from Dumfries to the Isle of Mull,[37] and the new 'e-organisation' craftscotland.

Craftscotland is perhaps the perfect exemplar of the economy and informa-tion pulses behind Scottish craft policy and activity. It is at one level a simple website: www.craftscotland.org. But in its first breathless year, craftscotland has become a truly dynamic portal.[38] It describes, writes about, hosts opinions on the crafts; it promotes and inspires craft practice, and the selling and distribution of craft objects. It is a democratic meeting place for ideas, images and specific craft content, relevant to Scotland, and viewed internationally. It hosts virtual exhibitions. Craftscotland aims to become an audience development agency for the crafts in Scotland, acting with technical sophistication and worldwide reach. It has the verve of the Australian website craft culture produced by Craft Victoria,[39] with the authority that derives from consensus, independence, and a shared vision. It has no parallel in England.

Seen from the vantage point of the south of England, but with an affectionate memory of my own spell as a specialist decorative art curator in a Scottish museum, what strikes me most about the contemporary craft infrastructure in Scotland is its unrealized potential. What has been done well – North Lands, craftscotland, commissioning for the public realm, the quiet and still unsung collection of craft for Scotland's museums – has often been done to international standards. Small organisations and relatively small-scale projects have shown both vision and determination. There is redoubtable energy and creativity, often against the odds, vested in a small number of 'craft champions' who have given sustained service to the sector. This ensures that in pivotal public and private galleries, within the Higher Education world, fairs, open studios, exhibitions and education projects, the crafts impinge imaginatively on the national conscience, and reflect the outstanding contribution to creative and economic life by the body of craft practitioners living and working in Scotland.

This is important, especially because of the opportunities that might be heralded by the next major policy shift, on the establishment of the new body Creative Scotland in 2008. If there are seismic shifts ahead, then the crafts can make a compelling case, backed up by real and virtual communities, replete with up-to-date information, for additional investment. Success and failure in the crafts ride a fine line. The re-emergence of the renowned Dovecot Studios, facing closure in 2002, to a new chapter as a sustainable business, acts as a reminder of this tight-rope act.[40]

As the report *Craft Businesses in Scotland* argued in 2002:

> Crafts enterprises can be very dynamic and aggressive in their explo-
> ration of difficult markets, and even enter the international stage as
> 'instant internationals' .... They make a contribution to artistic and
> technical innovation.[41]

The work that results from these small and micro businesses in Scotland reaches and enriches public collections and spaces. It is both a private and a public body of work, a national craft collection and national activity which are international in aspiration, grounded in the virtues of independence, dogged-ness, and the search for quality.

ABOUT THE WRITER

Simon Olding began his museum career at Glasgow Art Gallery and Museums, following on from his PhD researching the short story in the 1890s at the University of Edinburgh. He has held senior management and board positions in arts and museum organisations and is currently Director of the Crafts Study Centre, University College for the Creative Arts.

ACKNOWLEDGEMENTS

This essay could not have been written without the generous advice and comments of: Susie Alcock, Phillipa Aitken, Helen Bennett, Celia and Matthew Burt, Catriona Baird, James Coutts, Amanda Game, Juliet Kinchin, Lynn Park, Christine Rew, Tina Rose, Paul Stirton, Rose Watban and Rosemary Watt.

1 *Alexander Leckie* (St Enoch Exhibition Centre, Glasgow), 20 February to 28 March 1982.

2 Sir Harry Jefferson Barnes (1915-92) was Director of The Glasgow School of Art (1964-80).

3 *Alexander Leckie: ceramics* (Glasgow Museums and Art Galleries, 1982), p. 6.

4 Quoted in *Craftwork – Scotland's Craft Magazine* (Summer 1975), pp. 11-12.

5 The Scottish Development Agency was itself wound up in 1991, with its functions transferred to a new economic development agency, Scottish Enterprise. A new company, Made in Scotland Ltd, was set up with the brief to provide commercial services for craft businesses. See 'The visual arts and crafts', in *Cultural Trends in Scotland: 1995* (PSI), pp. 62-69.

6 See Juliet Kinchin and Andrea Peach: 'Small Pieces of Scotland: Souvenirs and the Good Design Debate 1946-80', in *Journal of the Scottish Society for Art History*, vol. 7, 2002, pp. 23-30.

7 Kinchin and Peach: p. 23. See also *Scottish Craft Centre: the first five years* (1955).

8 Richard Carr: 'Scottish crafts case', in *Crafts* (September/October 1990), p. 14.

9 See Tanya Harrod: *The Crafts in Britain in the Twentieth Century* (Yale University Press, 1999), pp. 462-63.

10 Richard Carr: 'Scottish craft upheaval', in *Crafts* (January/February 1991), p. 13.

11 www.craftscotland.org/aaswhatis.html

12 SAC funds for the crafts: £300,000 in 1993 (including overheads [grants to crafts in this first year were £137,818]);

£750,000 in 2003; £816,000 (grants only) in 2006.

13 See *Crafts* (March/April 1995), p. 12.

14 *Building Bridges: Scottish Arts Council support for crafts in Scotland 1993-2003* (Scottish Arts Council 2003).

15 *The real world: a prospectus for the crafts in the south west* (South West Arts 2002).

16 Conversation with Christine Rew, June 2006.

17 See Andrea Peach: 'Representations of Scottish Craft: *Craftwork Magazine* 1972-1988', a paper for the Design History Society Conference in 2002.

18 See *Ten years on 1992-2002: ten years of the Roger Billcliffe Gallery* (Roger Billcliffe Gallery 2002).

19 Conversation with Lynn Park, April 2006.

20 In 2002 The Scottish Gallery exhibited *16/16: 16 potters from 16 years*, a celebration of 16 years of selling contemporary crafts.

21 Artisan's three seasons were held in 1997, 1998 (in the Edinburgh International Conference Centre) and 2002 (George Heriot's School grounds). Festival Directors were Tony Gordon, Michael Dale and Richard Green.

22 Tony Gordon, in the Foreword to Artisan's first publicity brochure.

23 There were 100 makers in Artisan 02.

24 Edmund de Waal, in *Crafts* 155 (November/December 1998), p. 64.

25 The spirit of enterprise, characteristic of North Lands, is also at work in projects such as the Big Willow. This project was set up as an international master

class and exhibition by the Scottish Basket Makers Circle. The outcomes include a willow sculpture by the American maker Patrick Dougherty, along with a touring exhibition that started in Inverness in 2006.

26 In 2006 the relevant Higher Education Institutions are: Edinburgh College of Art; The Glasgow School of Art; Duncan of Jordanstone College of Art and Design, University of Dundee; Gray's School of Art, The Robert Gordon University, Aberdeen; School of Textiles and Design, Heriot-Watt University, Edinburgh. Cardonald College, Glasgow and Telford College, Edinburgh, are two examples of Scottish further education colleges running craft-based courses whose students have gone on to study at university level.

27 Tim Stead (1952-2000) produced many major installations such as the innovative *Peepshow* at the Gallery of Modern Art, Glasgow. He was a contributor to the Millennium Clock at the former Royal Museum, Edinburgh. See www.timsteadfurniture.co.uk

28 See Jane Heath (ed): *The furnished landscape: applied art in public places* (Bellew Publishing, Crafts Council, Arts Council 1992), p. 52.

29 Stephanie Brown: 'Commissions', *Crafts*, 139 (March/April 1996), pp. 16-19.

30 Burt made various items including café seating, a reception desk and tables. His 'welcome desk' for the An Tuireann Arts Centre was commended in the 2003 Saltire Society Arts in Architecture Awards.

31 Philippa Swann: 'Commissions', in *Crafts* 192 (January/February 2005), p. 27.

32 Swann, p. 29.

33 *Crafts*, 153 (July/August 1998), p. 17.

34 Trevor Walden, Director of Glasgow Museum and Art Galleries (1971-79). See *Glasgow Art Gallery and Museums: the building and collections* (Collins, 1987), p. 68.

35 See *Building a crafts collection: Crafts Council collection 1972-1985* (Crafts Council, 1985), pp. 196-97. A list of the 'major public collections of contemporary crafts in the UK' lists five collections in Scotland: Aberdeen Art Gallery & Museums; The Scottish Development Agency (for the Scottish Crafts Collection 'of approximately 200 pieces by makers resident in Scotland at the time the work was purchased'); the then Royal Scottish Museum, Edinburgh; Art Gallery and Museum, Glasgow; Paisley Museum and Art Gallery.

36 Other public venues which include crafts in their exhibition programmes include Dundee Contemporary Arts; the Bonhoga Gallery, Shetland; and the Dick Institute, Kilmarnock.

37 Nine craft development officers in Scotland are currently listed on the craftscotland website.

38 The website received 40,770 unique visitors in March 2006.

39 www.craftculture.org

40 David Weir is Managing Director of the new Dovecot Studios Limited.

41 *Crafts Businesses in Scotland: a study* (Scottish Enterprise Network; Scottish Arts Council 2002), p. 7.

Artist
Rachel Hazell

Born 1970, London, England

Training
1999-2001 MFA Printmaking
– Edinburgh College of Art
1997-98 MA Book art –
Camberwell College of Art,
London
1995-97 HND Book-binding –
London College of Printing
1990-95 MA (Hons) – The
University of Edinburgh

Inspiration
Stationery, repetition, architecture, landscape, design,
libraries

Tools and processes
Thinking, sketching, cutting,
measuring, folding, ripping,
gluing, pressing, waiting;
with scalpels, a slitting knife,
size-18 needle, braddle,
dividers, metal ruler, shears

Materials
Paper (esp. mould-made like
Somerset Velvet), grey board,
mill board, book cloth, pva,
waxed linen thread, watercolour ink, found objects

**Examples of work in
public collections**
Artlink Central, Stirling
Edinburgh International
   Book Festival, Scottish Arts
   Council
Manchester Metropolitan
   University
CitéCulture, Cité International-
   ale Universitare de Paris

Statement
'*A collection of pages = a
book.*

Creating books satisfies a
desire for order. Hand-binding
enables the topical arrange-
ment of "things", according
to current preoccupations.

'The scale of my work in-
creased when the Helen Storey
Foundation (2001) asked me to
design and build a two metre
high book sculpture, but small
personal books and specific
details remain important.

'The book form interests
me; particularly its place in
both real and imaginary
landscapes. While only a few
words may be included, they
are carefully chosen.

'Artist residencies in Shetland, on a Russian ice-breaker
in the Southern Seas, and in a
studio overlooking the Eiffel
Tower, have shaped both my
learning and ability to share.
Everyone has a book inside
them – these continue to be
drawn out; at school workshops, at festivals, on islands,
and at lighthouses!

'I want to move into working with the actual environment; envisioning enormous
land art pieces, spelling out
narratives across the "wide
white page" that is Antarctica.

'I love the way light and
shadow make pages sing.'

Artist Dorothy Hogg MBE

Born
1945, Troon, Ayrshire, Scotland

Training
1971-72 Moray House College of Education, Edinburgh
1967-70 Royal College of Art, London
1963-67 The Glasgow School of Art

Inspiration
'Inspiration comes from my subconscious and ideas take form through drawing and experimenting with materials.'

Tools and processes
The variety of traditional tools and techniques associated with jewellery and silversmithing.

Materials
Silver, gold, felt and mixed materials

Examples of work in public collections
Birmingham Museums & Art Gallery
National Museums Scotland, Edinburgh
The Koch Ring Collection, Germany
Musee Des Arts Decoratifs, Montreal

Statement
'My aesthetic is driven by my subconscious mind and reflects, in an abstract way, events and changes in my life. The structure of the body, its movements and related conscious and unconscious symbolic thoughts, preoccupy my design process.

'I work mainly in precious metal, and am fascinated by the way forms can be constructed in sheet metal to appear solid. Although the tube and sheet silver and gold forms I make imply density, they are in reality light as they are hollow and contain space. I attach symbolic value to the forms and to the use of colour.

'Parallel to making jewellery, I have been involved in education and have taught and assessed at various art institutions since 1972. For 21 years now I have been lucky enough to be Course Leader of the Jewellery and Silversmithing Department at Edinburgh College of Art. I am committed to ensuring that the progression from college to the professional world is more accessible to current students than it was to those of my generation.'

Artist
Adrian Hope

Born
1953, Edinburgh, Scotland

Training
1977 Postgraduate –
   Edinburgh College of Art
1975 Sheffield College of Art

Tools and processes
Raising, fabricating and
embossing

Materials
Silver, gold, copper, other
metals and wood

**Examples of work in
public collections**
Birmingham Museums & Art
   Gallery
National Museums Scotland,
   Edinburgh
Victoria and Albert Museum,
   London
Worshipful Company of
   Goldsmiths, London

Statement
'I think it is only human to
want to create something;
an object or a story; something useful; or something
to entertain.

   'At its best what we create
is in some way enlightening.
At its worst it is yet another
means of destruction.

   'It is my belief that since
creating almost anything
begins in the destruction of
something else, there is an
obligation to justify that and
make the very best I can.'

Artist
Sarah Keay

Born
1981, Dundee, Scotland

Training
1999-2003 BA (Hons)
   Jewellery and Silver-
   smithing – The Glasgow
   School of Art

Inspiration
Botanical elements (from sea
anemones to lacewing eggs
and tree branches)

Tools and processes
Wooden French knitting
bobbins

Materials
Silver, gold, precious and
semi-precious stones, crystals,
monofilament, enamel paint

Statement
'I knit enamelled wire tubes
that I then layer together to
create strong and durable
structures.

   'My creative practice is
heavily influenced by botanical elements that are re-
created and fragmented by
fabricated units constructed
from filament. Precious beads,
swarovski crystals, or found
objects are suspended by
enamel paint.

   'The repetitive techniques
used in the production of
the pieces are mirrored in
natural structures: tree
branches, lace-wing eggs,
sea anemones.

   'The pieces are designed
to allure and capture the
wearer using movement and
colour, blurring the margins
of nature and person, as well
as exploring the boundaries
between jewellery, textiles
and sculpture.

   'Utilisation of unconventional materials, alongside
ancient techniques, allows
my jewellery continually to
develop and diversify, whilst
also questioning the traditional roles of jewellery.'

*All is not gold
that glisteneth ....*
                    Thomas Middleton

Artist Sara Keith

Born 1969, Glasgow

Training
Studying for PhD Applied
  Art, Univ. of Dundee

2006-09 Duncan of Jordan-
  stone College of Art and
  Design, Univ. of Dundee
1986-90 BA (Hons)
  Embroidered and Woven
  Textile Design – The
  Glasgow School of Art

Inspiration Ethnographic
textiles, rituals, travel,
costume, beach-combings

Tools and processes
Shibori-shaped resist dyeing,
electroforming, hand and
machine-stitched manipul-
ated textiles

Materials Silk, cashmere,
cotton, linen, thread, buttons,
beads, silver, gold, precious
stones and found objects

Statement
'By using the process of
electroforming I can com-
bine the meticulous craft of
Shibori with silver; essentially
using silver in place of dye to
create pattern and form.
Some areas of the work are
transformed into solid silver,
where others are only par-
tially electroformed, exposing
areas of the original textile
underneath. Detail is created
by stitch marks "trapped" on
the concealed cloth, highlighted by rubbing back the
surface silver.'

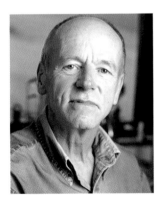

Artist Roger Morris

Born 1946, United Kingdom

Training
1972-75 Royal College of
  Art, London

1969-72 Central School of
  Art and Design, London

Inspiration
Fine Art, nature, ancient and
contemporary jewellery

Tools and processes
Lathe/milling machine,
electroformer, fabrication,
setting and riveting

Materials
Acrylic, stones, gold and
silver

**Examples of work in
public collections**
National Museums Scotland,
  Edinburgh
Victoria and Albert Museum,
  London
Houston Museum of Fine Arts,
  USA
National Gallery of
  Melbourne, Australia

Statement
'Current collaboration work
is heralding the emergence
of science-led work with a
challenging and exciting
design theme. Electroforming onto textile structures is
opening up enormous potential; in particular, being able
to manipulate shapes that
would be impossible to
create using conventional
metal techniques.'

Artist Alison Kinnaird MBE

Born
1949, Edinburgh, Scotland

Training
1970-71 Edinburgh College
of Art
Summer 1969
Workshop training with
Harold Gordon, Forres
1968-71 MA Celtic Studies
and Archaeology – The
University of Edinburgh

Tools and processes
Engraving on glass, using
copper-wheel engraving, sandblast and flexible drive
engraving, LED (light emitting
diodes) lighting and dichroic
colour

Materials
Optical glass panels

**Examples of work in
public collections**
Scottish National Portrait
Gallery, Edinburgh
Scottish Parliament,
Edinburgh
Victoria and Albert Museum,
London
Corning Museum of Glass,
Corning, New York, USA

Statement
'My work deals with the
illusory and transitory nature
of glass, which has such very
special qualities. Combing
several engraving techniques
allows a freer, more painterly
and expressive line, and a
larger scale than that possible with wheel engraving
alone. It pleases me to use
an ancient technique in a
modern context, especially
when it is enhanced by the
addition of LED lighting,
which brings a new impact
to the engraving.'

Artist
Andrew Lamb

Born
1978, Edinburgh, Scotland

Training
2002-04 MA Goldsmithing, Silversmithing, Metalwork and Jewellery – Royal College of Art, London
2000-01 Postgraduate Training Course/Residency – Bishopsland Workshops
1996-2000 BA (Hons) Silversmithing and Jewellery – Edinburgh College of Art

Inspiration
Nature, illusion, 'Op-Art' and textile techniques

Tools and processes
Laser-welder, tig-welder, wire drawbench and traditional goldsmithing techniques

Materials
White, yellow and red gold, silver

Examples of work in public collections
Decorative Art Collection of the City of Edinburgh
National Museums Scotland, Edinburgh
Worshipful Company of Goldsmiths, London
Galerie Marzee Collection, Nijmegen, The Netherlands

Statement
'Illusion and the mesmerising visual effects of Optical Art are significant influences in my jewellery. By incorporating these principals, I aim to create striking, yet delicately-shaped, pieces which appear to shift and change as they move across the eye.

'I also find inspiration in the linear patterns and structures abundant in nature and woven textiles. With these in mind, I use a combination of fine lengths of 18 ct gold and silver wire to construct sculptural, three-dimensional jewellery. The wire is layered, twisted or overlapping to create pieces with rippling textures and subtle colour changes with just the slightest of movements.

'The visual outcome is an enchanting illusion which is instant and endearing. My passion for jewellery is expressed in my continually evolving design process. I love using precious metals in a playful way that engage both the wearer and viewer in a moment of delightful surprise.'

Artist
Ann Little

Born
1973, Berwick-upon-Tweed,
Scotland

Training
1996 Postgraduate –
    Edinburgh College of Art
1991-95 Edinburgh College
    of Art

Inspiration
Natural forms, colour and
light of surroundings

Tools and processes
Enamelling, hand tools

Materials
Silver, enamel, slate and
cannel coal

**Examples of work in
public collections**
Aberdeen Art Gallery &
    Museums
National Museums Scotland,
    Edinburgh

Statement
'I work predominantly with
enamel and precious metals,
occasionally combining
natural materials such as
slate and cannel coal.

 'My work has gradually
become more sculptural,
developing from quite flat
pictorial pieces to more
sculptural forms.

 'Recent work has involved
enamelling onto squashed
or bent hollow forms. I am
interested in the combination
of the distressed forms

with the fragile enamel.

 'I work with a few hand
tools and use my hands and
the workbench to bend
and squash forms. Slate and
cannel coal is hand carved
and shaped using saws, files
and chisels.

 'The surface of my work is
very important. Enamel is
built up in layers, and much
time is spent rubbing the
enamel back to a matt finish,
making the enamel resemble
ceramic or stone. Inspiration
for my work is from my
immediate surroundings in
the Scottish Highlands, both
from the natural forms and
the colour and light.'

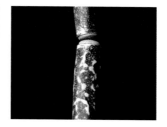

Artist
Michael Lloyd

Born
1950, Salisbury, England

Training
Royal College of Art, London

Inspiration
Natural and moral
philosophy

Tools and processes
Mainly hand raised and
chased – some constructed
vessels

Materials
Silver, copper, gold

**Examples of work in
public collections**
Ashmolean Museum, Oxford
Birmingham Museums & Art
  Gallery
National Museums Scotland,
  Edinburgh
Victoria and Albert Museum,
  London

Statement
'I am a compulsive maker and
a lover of nature and life.
  'My obsessions are currently
focused on making objects
that I like to define as
weapons of peace: from the
chalice to vessels for flowers,
a pursuit of forms that are
engaged with a fourth
dimension, beyond design
and decoration, into the
realms of spiritual enrich-
ment.'

Artist
Grant McCaig

Born
1974, Scotland

Training
1994-98 BA (Hons) Silversmithing and Jewellery –
The Glasgow School of Art

Tools and processes
Hammer raising vessels from
sheet metal

Materials
Sheet silver, copper, slate,
wood and found materials

**Examples of work in
public collections**
Birmingham Museums & Art
Gallery

Statement
'I have always been drawn
to the sea for some reason.
I suppose this is not such a
surprise when you discover
that I live on an island. Most
journeys in Britain, but in
particular Scotland, take in a
view of the North Sea or the
Atlantic, or an expanse of
water forming the mouth of
a river such as the River Forth.

'This contact, over time,
has become woven into my
work. Whether looking at
the objects that have been
washed up on the beach,
rounded, sanded, distressed
layers of paint flaking off to
reveal bare wood or foam; or
metal that has been tumbled
and forged by the rhythmic
pounding of the sea onto
rocks until it is transformed
and looks almost like bone,
bleached white and porous.
This in essence is what I want
to explore within this theme:
the potential for change and
metamorphosis within the
material and the object. The
idea of the object changing
over time fascinates me.

'Whether this is as a result
of handling by the owner,
or the materials themselves
changing (for example',
silver oxidizes in the form
of tarnish), ferrous metals
would eventually develop a
patina of rust and wood may
become darker when exposed
to the sun, or develop cracks
as seasoning takes place.

'This is not an enforced
change, but a gradual one
which in time gives us an
object of great personal
relevance and resonance.'

CLOSE TIES: FAR-FLUNG ...

A VIEW FROM AUSTRALASIA

Grace Cochrane

However can it be possible to comment on the significance of contemporary Scottish crafts from the perspective of the rest of the world? In the catalogue list for *The Cutting Edge* some of the people and their work are familiar, many are not. This selection reflects a number of different starting points. I recognize some directions that are, perhaps, international in their scope, and some that appear more regional in their reference. While old and new technologies are used, the work is not primarily to do with Scottish traditions or experiences, though some of these are reflected in the content and meaning of a number of pieces. How can I read this work?

A New Zealander in Australia with a Scottish name, I am sitting in the winter sunshine, in Sydney, listening to rosellas in the top of a gum-tree, reading these two companion essays which provide such excellent frameworks for understanding contemporary Scottish crafts. Yes, I do have a perspective of Scotland, albeit a comparatively distant one; but around the globe, with different experiences, other people of Scottish heritage would have very different things to say. After all, for every one of the five million people living in Scotland, most of whom identify as Scottish, we are told there are five more migrants or their descendants elsewhere in the world.

But perhaps the specific is in fact quite universal? We might all have a good deal in common. The offspring of migrants everywhere generally harbour some need to maintain links with their origins, and the more far-flung and difficult the connection, the stronger those desires may often be. Our perceptions of your present, in Scotland today, are tempered by our own experiences and imaginings of your past – but also as our heritage. And of course, in these places far-flung from where you are, there are many people whose origins have nothing to do with Scotland, and who have no reason to give it any special consideration at all.

Scottish influences are strong, however, in our part of the world. Subtle connections, often not immediately recognized, may yet have been much more pervasive than the obvious keeping of traditions than the efforts of the many

Caledonian and Celtic societies and festivals might indicate. We joke about Protestant work ethics – and continue to practice them. Where the Australian accent is said to have its foundations in Irish and Cockney sources, the New Zealand accent owes a great deal to Scottish migrants. Whatever their origin, all New Zealanders 'wait a wee while' or 'try a wee bit harder' now and again. We identify with fictional characters like Hamish Macbeth and Rebus; and when in 2005 Scottish-born Australian art critic Peter Hill wrote about his experience of taking a year off as an art student in Dundee to work as a lighthouse keeper on three islands on Scotland's west coast in the early 1970s, even those who had only seen these places in their imagination identified strongly with his story.[1]

The sounds of Scotland are also crucial to our perception of where you live and who you, and we, are. In 1992, when Michael Nyman composed the music for the award-winning New Zealand-made film *The Piano*, he said:

> Initially I was unsure as to how precisely to pitch the style. But … since Ada was from Scotland, it was logical to use Scottish folk and popular songs as the basis for our music …. It's as though I had to write the music of another composer who happened to live in Scotland, then New Zealand, in the mid-eighteen fifties.[2]

For today's Australasians, what used to be a two-year working holiday, travelling 'home' by ship to reconnect with places left by earlier generations, can now be much more brief and frequent experiences. For those connected in some way with the crafts, it is now possible to combine professional events with personal pilgrimages. In recent years, conferences like *Challenging Crafts* in Aberdeen in 2004, and residential workshops like those at North Lands Creative Glass in Lybster, have provided opportunities to connect with both the past and the present. And it is a most extraordinary experience to stand staring at stone cottages, or to walk through those small towns knowing that your forebears walked there also. Simon Olding earlier mentions the successful e-organisation craftscotland that 'has no parallel in England' (see page 64). Equally, the website scotlandspeople.gov.uk has few parallels in the world. Scotland's decision to place all parish records, census records and wills on a globally accessible site, makes it possible to print out documents handwritten well over a century ago.

While I visited the cottage in Glen Isla where I'd stayed with my great-aunt Grace some decades before, now the weekend home of ceramist Tony Franks, itself a coincidence, New Zealand glass artist Marea Timoko went off to seek antecedents of her Scottish father. Timoko, also with Maori heritage, had just completed a window and entrance-way to a *whare* (meeting house) on a *marae* (community meeting place), an unusual commission for a Maori woman. In a subsequent residency at Lybster in 2005, she found conceptual connections between the gateway of the *marae* and the flagstones and lintels of Scottish crofts, as well as the steps used by the fisherwomen of Whaligoe – influences that continue in her current work.

Events initiated or supported by organisations like the Scottish Arts Council, by museums and universities, and by regional groups like North Lands Creative Glass, bring many people from our part of the world, and elsewhere, to Scotland. Over the years many Australasians have visited Scottish schools of art, and have given workshops and lectures. Some schools, like the Australian National University School of Art, in Canberra, working with those in Glasgow, Dundee and Edinburgh, support student exchange programs; while the Scottish Executive of the British Council includes Australians and New Zealanders in offers of scholarships to undertake postgraduate study in Scotland. Many others make their own connections: Susan Wraight, a miniature-carver working in the Japanese netsuke tradition, was commissioned by the Marquis of Bute in 1991 to make carved components for a house interior. The Scottish Gallery has represented Australian metalworker Robert Foster since including him in *Collect* in

2006; while the work of ceramic artists Pippin Drysdale and Robin Best is included in the permanent collection of National Museums Scotland.

Scots also find their way to us. From the 1960s specialist crafts organisations provided effective information and international contacts; and by the early 1970s, following the lead of the American and British Crafts Councils, multi-crafts councils had formed in all Australian states, and in New Zealand. Since the establishment in 1973 of the federal funding body, the Australia Council for the Arts, which included the crafts for the first time,[3] the development of state arts funding bodies and the formation of Creative New Zealand,[4] there have been increasing exchanges of people and their work. Universities, museums and specialist crafts organisations hold conferences and summer schools, and speakers from all parts of the world, including Scotland, are invited. Your craftscotland website and our journals[5] bring your work to our attention. In recent years visitors have included Tony Franks from Edinburgh College of Art, Scottish-born Norman Cherry from the University of Central England in Birmingham, Sarah Hall and Archie McCall from The Glasgow School of Art, Gordon Burnett from Gray's School of Art in Aberdeen, and Paul Simmons from Timorous Beasties in Glasgow. Potter Fergus Stewart has moved between the two countries over at least 15 years.

This two-way connection is more than a recent experience. In the same way that Scotland has always had to define itself in relation to its southern neighbour, so the countries in Australasia have had to define themselves in relation to the northern hemisphere. Both Australia and New Zealand have continuing Indigenous societies, and there has always been a connection with Asia, but from the late eighteenth century it was the United Kingdom, and then Europe, which provided the greatest migrant populations. For much of this time the centre was seen to be elsewhere – at the point of origin. But what makes Australasian work significant internationally today is the way it has defined its own identity, strongly drawing on, but not hostage to, its many traditions.

Scots played a significant role in the general British colonial expansion of the nineteenth and early twentieth centuries, and in the settling of New Zealand in particular. The National Museum of Scotland in Edinburgh draws attention to the many stories of migration. While most *émigrés* went to North America, there were times when almost half came to Australia and New Zealand. Scots figured prominently as professional leaders, as well as commercial ones, as strong trading links were developed with the new colonies. And it was second-generation Scot, Andrew 'Banjo' Paterson, who in 1895 wrote the now famous Australian folk-song, 'Waltzing Matilda.' In New Zealand the colony's most distinctive Scottish settlement was in Otago, in the South Island, from 1848. The township was named Dunedin, the ancient Celtic name for Edinburgh, and it was here that New Zealand's first university, art school and college of education were established.

In the subsequent century and a half, whatever happened in Britain technologically and stylistically also happened in Australasia – the Arts & Crafts movement, Impressionism, Art Deco, Modernism, the contemporary crafts movement. Scottish connections continued. Jeweller Rhoda Wager moved to Sydney just before the end of the First World War, bringing the techniques and Arts & Crafts style of the Glasgow School to Australia. In 1989 her niece, Dorothy M. Wager (Judge), trained by her aunt, travelled to Scotland to meet Brian Blench from Glasgow Museums and to research her aunt's training and the origins of her work.

Some came to teach; others to work in industry and later to set up studios. Some were part of post-war migration programmes. With a Scottish diploma in Design and Art Teaching, Meg Douglas found employment in 1958 as a craft teacher at the School of Art in Adelaide and was influential in founding the Embroiderers Guild and the Craft Association of South Australia. Stained-glass artist David Saunders came to Australia in the 1960s to work at Standard Glass in Sydney, before establishing his own studio where he provided training for others. One of the most colourful and challenging visitors was Alexander (Alex) Leckie, who came from Scotland to Adelaide in South Australia for some years from 1955. He was one of the first to introduce work from a background of interest in Modernist sculptural forms, at a time when Bernard Leach's Anglo-Oriental example was most influential. And I notice that the young Simon Olding was around in Glasgow on his return!

As the crafts infrastructure developed in Australia, expert advice was sought from elsewhere. Belinda Ramson had worked in Scotland with tapestry weaver Archie Brennan at the Dovecot Studios in 1967 and for twelve months in 1973, and Brennan was subsequently invited to Australia in 1975 to work at the Australian National University in Canberra: 'I had only to be part of the cultural life of the University and be willing to talk about my work to those who were interested … my responsibility was only to create an awareness of tapestry.' At the same time he provided advice on the setting up of the Victorian Tapestry Workshop in Melbourne and returned in 1976 to consult on its establishment.[6] In the following years there were many exchanges between the two institutions, with Joan Baxter and Carol Dunbar amongst those who came to Australia. More recently, Australians Joy Smith and Hilary Green have worked on the tapestry project at Stirling Castle.

Meanwhile, town artist David Harding was brought from Scotland in 1982 to encourage interest in employing artists to work with local government. Metalsmith David Cruickshank, who trained at Gray's School of Art in Aberdeen, also arrived in Australia in 1982, and within his range of silver-smithing he has recently revisited the two-handled *quaich* bowl that he last made at art school. Ceramist Malina Monk, from the Isle of Lewis, trained in Glasgow and came to Australia in 1969; and after study in Glasgow and Manchester, textile designer and consultant Bruce Carnie came to teach and later design for industry in 1981.[7] David Band, textile designer and artist, in Melbourne from 1986, and Sydney-based embroiderer and teacher Emma Robertson, from the

1990s, have also established significant careers here. In New Zealand Deborah Crowe, working between visual arts and fashion, trained in textile design and came from Glasgow in 1986.

Whether as recent migrants, or descendants of migrants, those who form part of the Scottish diaspora are as conscious of stereotyping as those who might be concerned about it in Scotland. Earlier generations worked hard to maintain their customs, while later ones integrated, though always conscious of their ties. Many make their work using the skills in which they were trained in Scotland, yet their work might equally reflect an anonymous internationalism or make reference to wherever they now live. Australians are equally determined to dismiss any myth that they are all sun-bronzed surfers or characters in *Neighbours*, or that their work will automatically reflect the Australian-ness of 'the outback'. Migrants from other countries have just as many, if not more, stereotypes to deal with. It is, nonetheless, for all a very rich and rewarding experience to sit between a place of origin (even some generations distant) and a place of residence or birth, and 'belong' to both. Those with Scottish heritage are no different; textile artist Jill Kinnear speaks of this as a 'third space'.[8]

Known for her printed textiles and award-winning public art works, Kinnear is a graduate in textile design from Duncan of Jordanstone College of Art, Dundee and the University of Southern Queensland. She is currently researching, through textiles, her experience as a migrant: 'I was one of the 152,000 people who left Scotland in the decade 1976-86, I was one of the approximately two million who left the country in the 20th century, and I was one of the many skilled and educated workers who have left Scotland in their thousands over centuries.' For an exhibition *Diaspora: Mapping migration in textiles*, she is combining and constructing metal elements and taking them to the departure lounge at Brisbane International Airport to be passed through the baggage X-ray machine, symbolic of transition from one country to another. The projected renditions are saved to a CD-rom as the basis for computer-generated images for digital prints,

reconfigured as 'tartans' and 'paisleys' in silk, cotton and wool for furnishings and wearables.

> I am interested in … how tartan imagery has migrated along with its mythologies …. Tartans conjure among the public at large an impression of overbearing nationalism …. But the story … is fascinating, the designs are often beautiful, they constitute an important facet of Scottish history and, cheap tourist paraphernalia aside, shrewd economic survival.[9]

Tapestry weaver Valerie Kirk also reflects a particular path of migration. Born in Dumfriesshire, she trained in art and design at Edinburgh College of Art in the 1970s, and visited Australia as a guest artist before settling here in 1987.[10] Kirk has undertaken some major tapestry commissions and has also led groups into Asia to research textile traditions. While considering issues of her own migration in response to Australia's social and cultural history, and sometimes using the motif of a salmon as a metaphor for her own journey, Kirk also refers to her own textile traditions. At various times she might draw on memories of a quilt of Scottish tweed and plaid suiting samples made within her own family, or details of nineteenth-century Ayrshire needlework, while at the same time looking at the constellation of the Southern Cross in the Antipodean sky, the 'making-do' quilts of pioneering women, or the coverings of pine-needles from the 'migrant' forests that join the native eucalypts around Canberra.[11]

Meanwhile, glass artist Elizabeth McClure, from Lanarkshire, studied at Edinburgh College of Art in the late 1970s and first visited New Zealand for a year in 1987. She taught in Australia from 1988, returning to live in Auckland in 1993.[12] Working on her own blown forms as well as found glass vessels, McClure cuts and engraves the surfaces, intrigued by the idea of mark-making as identification. 'In the last few years,' she says, 'I have crossed oceans and hemispheres and seasons, and this has profoundly affected my perception and interpretation .... Undoubtedly, [continued exposure to new colours in the Pacific light is] linked to the transition.'[13]

Also in Auckland, fashion designer and textile artist Miranda Brown is developing her new season's range for New Zealand Fashion Week 2006. With a background of designing and making costumes in film studios for *Xena: Warrior Princess* and *Lord of the Rings*, she specializes in working with shibori-dyed New Zealand merino wool fabric. The new range is geometric in its motifs:

> I am calling my new designs *Pacific tartan*. After all, I am a flaming red-head – my heritage is Celtic, and I am proud of it – and I am also working with Asian textile traditions, here in New Zealand. I am inspired by our Pacific surrounds and the tribal nature of Scottish and Pacific Island people. I am simply describing our tribes through our cloth.[14]

While risking the perpetuation of yet another stereotype, I do believe Australians and New Zealanders are characteristically resourceful and independent. They have limited local markets and are far from other centres. Like their counterparts described by Simon Olding in relation to the Scottish Arts Council's *Building Bridges* report,[15] they have to be inventive in finding paths that allow creative expression alongside sustainable ways of working.

I see *The Cutting Edge: Scotland's Contemporary Crafts* as an inspired core collection of current Scottish sensibilities that has noticeable extensions in our part of the world; extensions that reflect not only considerable transferred experiences from Scotland, but also imaginative negotiations in the best possible way between two important viewpoints – a place of origin and a place of residence.

ABOUT THE WRITER

Grace Cochrane is a freelance writer and curator, formerly Senior Curator, Australian Decorative Arts and Design, at the Powerhouse Museum, Sydney. She is currently Editor of *Object* magazine, and is organising an exhibition and symposium, *Smart Works: Design and the handmade*, for the Powerhouse Museum.

1 Peter Hill: *Stargazing: Memoirs of a Young Lighthouse Keeper* (Vintage edition, Random House: Sydney 2003).

2 For Michael Nyman, see: http://www.fys.uio.no/~magnushj/Piano/sound.html

3 Australian Council for the Arts, established 1968, re-formed in 1973; name changed to Australia Council for the Arts in 1975.

4 Creative New Zealand, 1994, was originally the Queen Elizabeth II Arts Council, established in 1964.

5 Journals like *Ceramics Art and Perception, Craft Arts International, Textile Fibre Forum* and *Object*, and the on-line publication from Craft Victoria, www.craftculture.org/

6 Brennan also ran two teaching workshops in 1976, in New South Wales and Victoria, which influenced a considerable number of weavers.

7 For much of the information here, see Grace Cochrane: *The Crafts Movement in Australia: a History* (University of North South Wales Press: Kensington 1992).

8 Jill Kinnear: 'The Familiar Stranger; mapping migration through textiles', an unpublished PhD thesis in progress (University of Southern Queensland, Toowoomba 2006). The third space is a term used by Homi Bhabha in H. K. Bhabha: *The Location of Culture* (Routledge: London 1994).

9 Kinnear: ibid.

10 Since 1991 Kirk has been Head of Textiles and a Senior Lecturer at the Australian National University School of Art, Canberra.

11 See Grace Cochrane in S. Walker, A. Brennan, G. Cochrane: *Portfolio Collection: Valerie Kirk* (Telos Art Publishing: Winchester 2003).

12 McClure taught at Australian National University School of Art, Canberra and was President of Ausglass 1991-93.

13 See Grace Cochrane, catalogue essay, in *Elizabeth McClure: Seasons of Change,* Dowse Art Museum, Lower Hutt, New Zealand 2001.

14 Conversation with author, July 2006.

15 See Simon Olding chapter in this book: 'A rightful place in the scheme of things: a history of craft resources in Scotland', on page 55.

Artist Helen McPherson

Born 1976 Lanark, Scotland

Training
2000-04 BA (Hons) Silver-
    smithing and Jewellery –
    The Glasgow School of Art

Inspiration
'I am drawn to contrasts in
pattern found in the agricul-
tural landscape. The interaction of man-made forms,
constructions and lines with
the natural landscape and the
resulting manipulation of the
flora and fauna, offers end-
less inspiration.'

Tools and processes
'I use a combination of traditional jewellery fabrication
techniques in combination
with new technology such as
the laser-weld and Rhino 3-D
computer technology.'

Materials
Precious metals, such as silver,
18 ct yellow gold, and semi-
precious stones are combined
with non-precious materials
such as slate, dried flower
heads, wool, threads, etc.

Statement
'I am interested in contrast …
of colour, shape and form.
By living and working from
my studio on the farm, my
surroundings are a constantly
changing, contrasting environment, as nature responds
to farming processes and
seasonal changes …. I love
the starkness of strong wire
fence lines, interspersed with
climbing plants and grasses.
Also, changes of light and
shade intrigue me; they project abstract, fragmented, flat

patterns on the ground below.
    'By harnessing traditional
jewellery and silversmithing
practices with new technologies such as laser-welding,
I can increase the possibilities
of contrasts in materials, fabrication and construction of my
work. The heat-free process
of laser-welding allows for a
finger-tip precision in construction and containment
of natural materials, such as
sheep wool, within a solid
metal structure. Oxidization
of silver creates a blackened
finish contrasting with bright
18 ct yellow gold plating;
smooth polished metal mir-
rors the rough, filed surfaces
of carved stone and slate.
    'Just as the natural world
is never entirely still, neither
is my work, each piece incorporating kinetic moveable
parts which respond to the
wearer's activity. My work
is an abbreviated summary
of the surrounding world:
a wearable, tactile, visual,
mobile, abstracted represen-
tation of the natural world.'

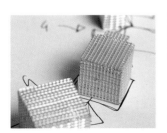

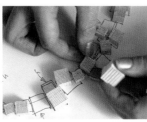

Artist
Jan Milne

Born
1972, Scotland

Training
1990-94 BA (Hons) Printed
    Textile Design – The
    Glasgow School of Art

Inspiration
Fruit, flowers, nature, colour

Tools and processes
Textile printing techniques,
laminating

Materials
Acrylic, fabrics

Examples of work in public collections
The Glasgow Collection
Home Office, London
Royal Botanic Gardens Café,
    Wales
Samba Grill, Mirage Casino,
    Las Vegas

Statement
'I graduated in Printed Textile Design in 1994 from Glasgow School of Art and founded the company in 1995 supplying custom printed textiles to architects and interior designers for use in both contract and domestic interiors.

'The initial "janmilne collection" soon established the company's identity of large-scale photographic fruit and flower imagery with use of vibrant colour.

'This signature style is also applied to digitally-printed laminates and to acrylics: this latest is available as nests of tables, wall panels, screens/room dividers and now dining tables and chairs.

'My designs are bright and bold, yet have a simplicity. The key strength of the designs is the expertise with which colour and placement are combined.

'My work has become recognized by architectural and interior design firms across the world, and many prestigious contracts have been received: New York's Fifth Avenue, "Genki Sushi"; projects with New York's Rockwellgroup; printed fabrics for the "Samba Grill" restaurant in the Mirage Casino, Las Vegas; Gloria Estefan's "Bongos" in Miami; fabric for New York's "W Hotels"; and "Fidelias" restaurant within the Mohegan Sun Casino, Connecticut where janmilne supplied fabric and vinyl for seating and printed laminates for tabletops.'

Artist
Keiko Mukaide

Born
1954, Tokyo, Japan

Training
1996 Workshop and
    conference – North Lands
    Creative Glass
1994 Bild-Werk Frauenau,
    Germany
1993 Sars-Poteries, France
1991 MA des Ceramic and
    Glass – Royal College of
    Art, London
1976 BA (Hons)
    Communication Design –
    Musashino Art University,
    Japan

Inspiration
Location/energy of places

Tools and processes
Various tools

Materials
Glass, metal

**Examples of work in
public collections**
The Crafts Council, London
Fitzwilliam Museum,
    Cambridge
Victoria and Albert Museum,
    London
Corning Museum of Glass,
    New York

Statement
'The modern devices are
convenient and compact, but
the old machines suggest an
anticipation of the future
while also retaining a visual
beauty.
   'Glass compasses are
objects which offer some
insight for the audience in
considering their own
location and life direction.'

Artist
Laura Murray

Born
1974, Elgin, Scotland

Training
1999 Masters of Design
(Textiles) – The Glasgow
School of Art
1992-96 BA (Hons) Silversmithing and Jewellery –
The Glasgow School of Art

Inspiration
Nature

Tools and processes
Textile and jewellery tools
and processes

Materials
Silver, ribbons, feathers, rope
and found objects

Statement
'I make one-off luxury bags
and sporrans; each one is
hand-crafted using mixed
media such as silver, ribbons,
feathers, ropes and found
objects.

'My work lies somewhere
between textiles and jewellery.

'Inspiration can come from
birds; their elegant shape or
the movement of a beak has
influenced the way some of
my bags open.

'Recent work includes a

range of sporrans: these are
seen as fun showcase pieces.
A work called "Pom Pom"
sporran is made from pink
strong rope. The pom poms
fly around when dancing!

'Another is made of felt-tip
pens, the coloured tubes and
felt-tip tops are inventively
used to create long tassels.

'This work was inspired by
a need to re-invent a traditional sporran, and also the
result of a residency with a
group of schoolchildren,
where their light-hearted
and open-minded approach
to design made me question
how I work.'

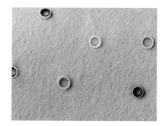

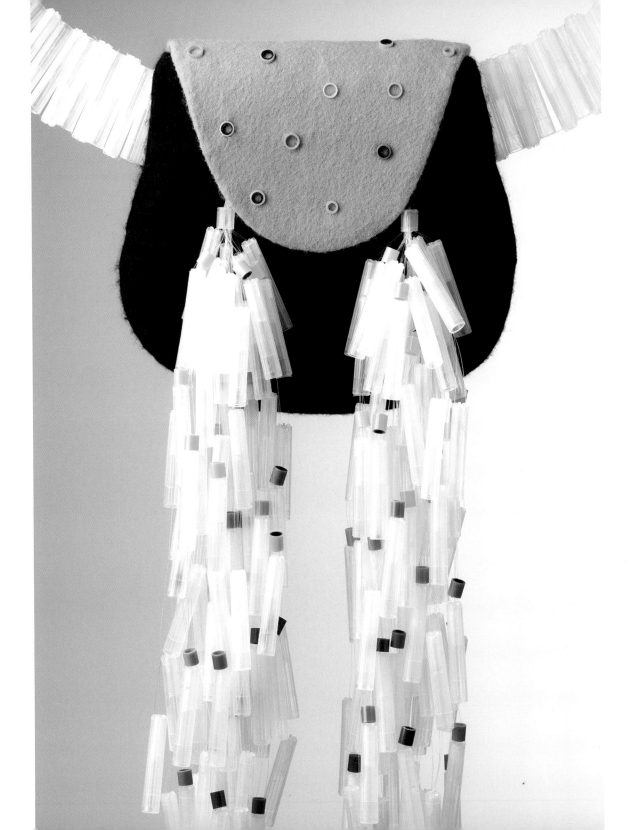

Artist Mai Therese Ørsted

Born
1970, Copenhagen, Denmark

Training
2002 Master class – Haystack
    Mountain School of Crafts,
    USA
2001 Concentration – Pen-
    land School of Crafts, USA
1998 Artist in Residence –
    North Lands Creative Glass
1997 MA Art & Design –
    Univ. of Wolverhampton
1996 BA (Hons) 3-D Design –
    Univ. of Wolverhampton
1994 Apprentice glassmaker
    – Orrefors Glas Skolan,
    Sweden

Inspiration
'Everything around me; both
nature and man-made
objects.'

Tools and processes
Digital technology and its
application to traditional
glass-making

Materials
Glass and metals

**Examples of work in
public collections**
North Lands Creative Glass,
    Lybster
Glasmuseum Ebeltoft,
    Denmark

Statement
'My aim in undertaking this
project is to move the boundaries for expression in craft
and design. My background
is founded in traditional
skills such as hand-cutting
and blowing glass. However
I find the aesthetics that my
present skills, and what glass
as a material will allow,
somewhat restricting. I wish
to add computer technology
and information about
mechanical cutting tech-
niques to my palette of
"hands-on" craftsmanship.
'The aim is to transfer both
computing, water, and laser-
cutting skills onto future
works in order to steer off
a path of traditional and
conventional production
methods, as these have a
fundamental impact on the
aesthetics of the final
design.
'However, the final piece
will combine old and new
techniques, as glass-blowing
and diamond-cutting will be
integrated.
'As an artist I find it help-
ful to use modern working
processes to take ancient
materials a step further and
to expand consistently what
is achievable. This is due to
human curiosity, but it also
stems from an urge to have
total control over the final
product. In my present working situation I find that my
education in traditional skills
sometimes can be limiting
for the design process.'

Artist
Stephen Richard

Born 1943, Junction City,
Kansas, USA

Training
2005 Master class with Klaus
Moje – North Lands
Creative Glass, Lybster
2002 Bohle courses on
Fusing and (2004) Finishing
1996 Glasgow College of
Building and Printing
1985-88 University of Wales,
Aberystwyth
1966 University of
Strathclyde, Glasgow
1960-64 University of
Kansas, USA

Inspiration
'Those who have gone before;
colleagues; the natural and
the built environments; childhood; overheard conver-
sational phrases; poetry.'

Tools and processes
Kilns, glass-cutters, knives,
wet-belt sanders, lathes,
saws, lap-grinders, moulds

Materials
Glass, paints, fibreboard,
investment materials, metals

**Examples of work in
public collections**
Corries Solicitors, Glasgow
Glasgow City Council
Little Italy, Glasgow
Scottish Football Association

Statement
'There is continuing dialogue
between me and the glass.
Both have capabilities that
need to be understood and
developed … unpredictabil-
ities that can be exploited.
Working with glass and incorporating other materials can
be a highly technical process.

It is the interaction of all
these elements that provides
me with the excitement
while working with glass.
    'Colour and the action of
lights on glass are major considerations for me in making
glass objects. Glass obscures,
reveals, reflects and colours
the living environment. A
sheet of glass together with
light can subtly alter the view.
It can reflect (actually and
metaphorically) the location,
or simply obscure the view,
reducing it to colour inter-
actions. As a reflective object
it can provide colour, light,
wonder, even humour.
    'I continue to try to "mine"
my childhood experiences to
provide innocent and naïve
approaches to social and
political situations and events.
My reaction to landscape
(built and natural) is at both
the microscopic and naturally
visible scales. Scientific developments from microscopic to
the astronomical, and the
associated knowledge, continue to stimulate me into
different approaches.'

Artist Sarah-Jane Selwood

Born
1969, Edinburgh, Scotland

Training
1991-92 Postgraduate
Diploma – Edinburgh
College of Art
1987-91 BA (Hons) Ceramics
– Edinburgh College of Art

Inspirations
Materials and processes

Tools and processes
Wheel-thrown, cut and altered
terracotta or porcelain clay,
high-fired to 1260°C, and
hand-diamond polished

Materials
Terracotta or porcelain clay

**Examples of work in
public collections**
Aberdeen Art Gallery &
Museums
Victoria and Albert Museum,
London
Museo Internazionale delle
Ceramiche Faenza, Italy
Takeo City Culture Hall
Takeo, Kyushu, Japan

Statement
'From wet clay on the wheel
to hard ceramic after firing,
the journey a pot takes
always inspires me. My work
has an alchemy both through
its physical transformation
and its design concept.
'To start, a perfect thrown
form, the fluidity of the soft
clay controlled and the pro-
portions and ultimate character of the piece are defined.
Next, the simple bowl is reconstructed, an origami of
clay created … cut, inverted,
rejoined … cut, inverted,
rejoined … a rhythm of lines
cascade from the rim creating
movement and disrupting
the internal and external
volumes of the perfectly-
formed bowl. Repeated cut
lines in the limit become new
curves within the form. The
method is calculated and
must be performed with
precision, yet the outcome
always surprises and the
element of risk and chance
remains.
'I work within a set of
self-imposed constraints,
rules which I can challenge
and stretch, but whose
structure continues to offer
limitless possibilities. In this I
find an analogy with baroque
music: Bach or Telemann
demonstrate a wealth of
ingenuity, the latent possibilities in a regular rhythmic
pattern, complex chords,
based on mathematical for-
mulae. Creativity flourishes
with a set of boundaries to
challenge.'

Artist
Sarah Taylor

Born
1969, Halifax, England

Training
1993-95 MPhil – Heriot-Watt
    University, Galashiels
1991-92 Postgraduate
    Diploma in Textile Design –
    Heriot-Watt University,
    Galashiels
1988-91 BA (Hons) in Textile
    Design – Winchester
    School of Art
1987-88 Foundation
    Certificate – Calderdale
    College of Further
    Education, Halifax

Inspiration
Unconventional, light-sensitive yarn types; transparency; movement; light; lighting products and materials

Tools and processes
Hand-weaving; shuttles

Materials
Optical fibres; nylon monofilament; paper; enamelled wire; light projectors

Examples of work in public collections
National Maritime Museum,
    Greenwich

Statement
'My work explores fibre optic technology within textiles and related artefacts.

'Since 1995, after discovering that the weaving process caused sufficient light loss along the length of end-glow optical fibres, I have continued to exploit the light-emitting properties of these fibres and commercial lighting devices through the medium of weave. Recent collaborations with sound and sensor experts have also produced interactive, multi-sensory artwork designed to stimulate hearing and touch as well as sight.

'The use of unconventional yarn types, particularly light-sensitive yarns in conjunction with optical fibres, are fundamental to my work and drive my desire to explore new fabric properties. Weaving with light allows me to create different colour moods, colour and lighting effects, eg polychromatic effects, which give the appearance of movement.

'The juxtaposition of yarn, structure, light and lighting device allows me to create programmable artefacts that are capable of stimulating or calming the senses through subtle or dramatic effect within controlled lit environments.

'Future work will continue to focus on the innovative use of technologies and craft-based processes where traditional techniques meet state of the art equipment.'

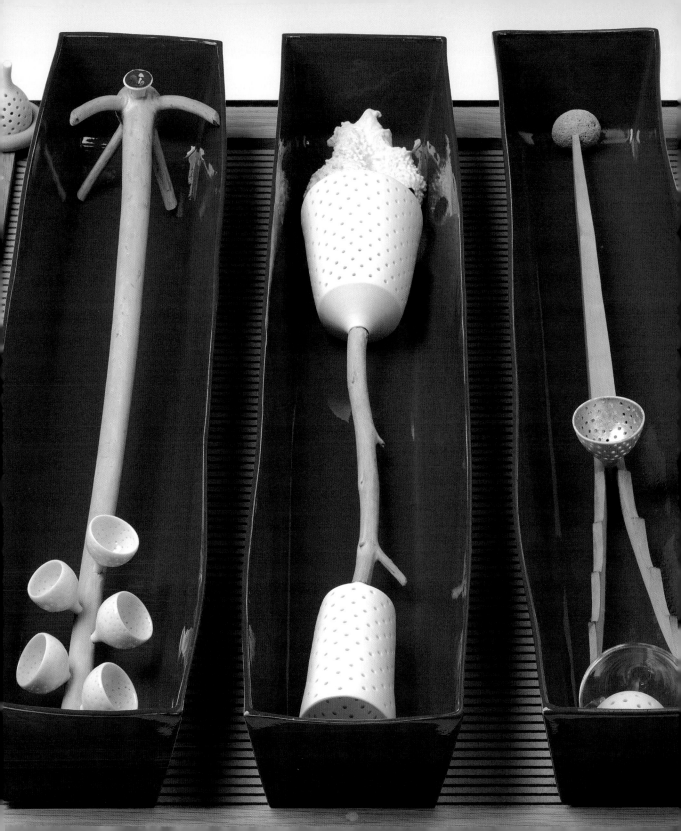

Artist
Simon Ward

Born
1964, Newmarket, England

Training
1995-97 Teaching Certificate – The Robert Gordon University, Aberdeen
1990-92 Masters, Ceramics and Glass – Royal College of Art, London
1985-88 BA (Hons) Ceramics – South Glamorgan Institute, Cardiff
1984-85 Foundation – Hastings College of Arts and Technology

Inspiration
'Primarily cultural exchange and indigenous crafts, specifically tools and implements relating to dining and working the land. Natural environment, location and the ephemeral, including collections of objects and materials.'

Tools and processes
'I utilize a mix of ceramic processes and tools. Process involves primarily throwing and slip-casting. Tools include off the shelf and home-made using found materials.'

Materials
Porcelain; wood, mainly oak; found materials – driftwoods, stone, other organic materials; metals like brass and silver

Examples of work in public collections
McManus Galleries & Museum, Dundee
World Ceramics Biennale, Icheon, South Korea
International Workshop of Ceramic Art, Tokoname, Japan
Mino collections, Seto, Japan

Statement
'Over the past five years my work has been primarily concerned with challenging the roles and context of porcelain in the interior and exterior environments. This has occurred through cross-cultural exchange via residency programmes in Japan and Europe, resulting in exhibitions in galleries, museums, restaurants and permanent site-specific large-scale sculpture.

'As a result of these exchanges, location and certain aspects of traditional indigenous craft-making have informed the research investigation through material collaboration.

'Forming connections and relationships between porcelain and wood, metal, concrete and other found materials has resulted in work which challenges the role of this material and its potential current/future contexts.'

IS SCOTTISH CRAFT

REALLY SCOTTISH?

David Revere McFadden

When I was invited to contribute a short essay to the publication that accompanies the exhibition *The Cutting Edge: Scotland's Contemporary Crafts*, it gave me an opportunity to think about questions of national identity in a time of globalized culture. Can one distinguish a national 'voice' in the work of artists in metal, glass, fibre, clay, from a particular geographic location? Specifically, is there is anything quintessentially 'Scottish' about the works selected and commissioned for *The Cutting Edge*, or are these works more realistically informed by much larger international forces that have influenced both the creation and the consumption of craft objects in the past few decades? And, if there is something Scottish about these works, how does anyone begin to define what is visually and culturally Scottish today?

For those of us who have been fortunate enough to be involved in the world once comfortably called 'craft', it has been exciting to observe the shifts in perception and practices that have taken place in the fields of metal, glass, fibre, clay and wood in the past two decades. During this time it has been impossible to ignore the energy and diversity that has propelled a new synthesis among the heretofore isolated and hierarchical worlds of art, craft and design. We are experiencing a critical shift in the ways studio-made objects of aesthetic value function in our world, a shift that has, to my own mind, created a genre of objects (and makers, for that matter) that are highly interdisciplinary, experimental and innovative. In conversation with myself, Victoria and Albert Museum design historian and educator Glenn Adamson once proposed that studio-made objects today might best be described as post-disciplinary in their rejection of traditional categories.[1] The more one looks over the international scene, the more this description seems to apply. And, as California College of the Arts President Michael Roth said of the new generation of students currently enrolled, they are often less wedded to a single medium than their predecessors, and move amongst mediums with ease. Roth described these new creators and makers as 'promiscuous' in their attitude toward materials and techniques.[2] This phenomenon is not limited to any specific country, but is truly international. In *The Cutting Edge*, basketry specialist Lizzie Farey experiments with lighting, Rachel Hazell uses sheet metal in lieu of paper for her sculptural book, and Sara Keith and Roger Morris (textile artist and metalsmith respectively) collaborate on applying metal-working technologies to textile structures, to cite only three examples. From Detroit to Dumfries, makers are breaking down barriers that have kept craft insular and retrospective. The world of today's studio makers is bigger and more challenging than ever. Combined with the instantaneous access to ideas and images provided by the internet, makers today are conversing easily with their peers, with experts from other disciplines, and with a global audience.[3]

This being said, the question of whether or not there is something uniquely Scottish about the works in *The Cutting Edge* still begs an answer. The question is not one that needed a great deal of attention in the world of so-called traditional crafts in Scotland. In 2000 National Museums Scotland organized and circulated *Celebrating Scotland's Crafts*.[4] The exhibition highlighted those craft traditions that are most often stereotypically identified with Scotland – tartans, bagpipes, traditional boats. Taken as a whole, these craft traditions were informed by what essayist Hugh Cheape described as 'elements such as geography, available resources and materials, and regional economies and the dynamics of the community'.[5] By comparison, the makers included in *The Cutting Edge* tend to be urban dwellers rather than rural. They have substantial higher education, rather than being self-taught, or are descendants of craftspeople working in the same field, who produce work that is negotiated as a commodity in an culture-based economy often driven by private and public commissions, museum curators, commercial galleries, the press and other media.

Curiously, the crafts profiled in *Celebrating Scotland's Crafts* were, to a large extent, fibre- and wood-based traditions – weaving and knitting, wood-carving and joinery, musical instrument-making. No mention was made of metalwork or jewellery, even though Scotland has maintained a dynamic tradition in the metals for centuries. Nor were ceramics or glass included. By comparison, metalworkers of one type or another dominate the artist roster in *The Cutting Edge,* followed by half as many each from the worlds of textiles and glass, with ceramics and mixed media touched upon only lightly. Whether or not this distribution can be taken as a demographic study of the preferred mediums in Scotland today is less important than the fact that these makers were selected by the curatorial team as representative of the new Scottish crafts. As an outsider looking in on this preselected world, it is especially important to look carefully at the works and makers in an effort to glean some ideas of trends, issues and concerns that engage creative Scottish makers today. In this essay I will look at each of the mediums individually, and offer a highly tentative preview of work being created for the exhibition.

Malcolm Appleby has had a long and distinguished career in metalwork, and has produced work of exceptional diversity, sometimes made in collaboration with other metalsmiths, and frequently highlighting his virtuoso talent as an engraver. He has executed an extraordinary number of private and public commissions for trophies, medals, centrepieces, and regalia. His work reflects his interest in new technologies, his deep appreciation of historical metalwork, and his distinctively witty sense of humour. To a great extent Appleby is the perpetuator of the long tradition of finely-crafted hollow ware with which Scotland is identified, and he frequently cites historical forms in his ceremonial pieces, such as his commemorative bowls.[6] Appleby subverts the history of his own chosen medium to comment on issues ranging from history and culture to the environment and contemporary politics. For Appleby and several others of the makers in *The Cutting Edge,* history in general, and Scottish history in particular, provides a rich library of ideas for new and innovative work.

A spirit of play and whimsy also infects the work of Ruth Chalmers, whether in the form of her calligraphic wirework studies of birds, or in her assemblages of metal and mixed medium clothing and animals from a Lilliputian world. Chalmers has also specialized in creating nonsensical automata, such as a wind-

up dog that walks itself, or a bracelet upon which a dog chases a permanently untouchable red ball suspended just in front of his muzzle. Whether or not humour of this variety can be said to have any particularly Scottish twist, it is undeniably a part of the current artistic landscape. A similar vein of whimsy pervades works by Jack Cunningham, who combines proficiency in traditional techniques of carving and silversmithing with unexpected imagery derived from nature. Andrew Lamb creates perceptually ambiguous wearable shapes – necklaces, bracelets and rings – that toy with our senses of vision by creating illusions of space, depth and movement. These works are not intentionally humourous, but they nevertheless engage the viewer in a spirit of play.

Ann Little uses often unexpected materials in her work in addition to the standard silver, gold and gemstones. More commonplace materials such as copper or slate are transformed into objects that suggest that the value of these materials has been grossly overlooked. For *The Cutting Edge* Little is creating works made from cannel coal, a clean-burning bituminous coal. Humility in materials, humour in attitude, and elegance in execution, are seamlessly merged in Little's work. Transforming ordinary materials into high drama theatre is the speciality of Peter Chang. Like Malcolm Appleby, Chang is of a slightly older generation than the majority of artists in the exhibition. Chang did his graduate studies in sculpture, which helps to explain his love affair with often bizarre and always colourful and memorable form. One does not wear a Peter Chang bracelet; it wears the wearer. Made of inherently worthless plastics and resins, Chang's fanciful shapes and brilliant colours and textures seem to have emerged from a children's storybook about an alien world inhabited by plants and creatures never seen on earth. Chang's humour and playfulness, however, never overpowers his sense of form and pattern, and it is this characteristic that makes his jewels into classics of post-Modernism.

While Ruth Chalmers' and Jack Cunningham's jewellery can be seen as a distant relative of the narrative jewellery produced by many American jewellers, and Chang's bold wearables as studies in dynamic colour and pattern, other Scottish silversmiths pursue another tributary in jewellery design – that of abstraction. Grant McCaig is well known for his pure studies of shape in vessels. While he is not averse to citing natural forms in some works – seaweed, shells, plants, fruits – it is his studies of abstract geometric form and essays in pure colour that stand out. Adrian Hope has likewise produced a body of work notable for the refinement and understatement of forms and textures. Helen McPherson's work is intricate yet simple, often comprised of small geometric elements that are repeated in staccato compositions. Small squares or cubes of metal, strung together to hang freely in space, become small references to architecture. For this exhibition McPherson has produced two neckpieces of varying length that support a series of metal cubes of different sizes.

Somewhere in the middle ground between the narrative/pictorial approach and the purely abstract is the jewellery sculptor Dorothy Hogg. I first became familiar with Hogg's work through the exhibition *100% Proof* which profiled many of Scotland's most versatile and accomplished studio jewellers.[7] Hogg's designs suggest, but in no way mimic, the world of nature. The stems and roots of plants or blood veins in the human body are poetically evoked in her forms, an effect underscored by her frequent use of brilliant blood-red felt and coral to fill small passages on the pieces.

The jewellery artists in *The Cutting Edge* reveal their affinities with jewellery design in other parts of the world, particularly those in the United States. Narrative and imagery, re-valuation of valueless materials, and a sense of humour, could be said to be an international platform. However, I do not believe that one would ever confuse these Scottish works with contemporary studio jewellery from the Netherlands, Italy or Japan. Running throughout these works is a sense of lightness and wit that stimulates the viewer to interact on a very personal level. Scottish jewellery is not driven by display, nor by the vagaries of fashion. It has indeed found its own voice.

The history of studio glass since the 1960s is one that includes what are now many national traditions. Many of today's traditions in art glass grew out of the massive renaissance of interest in studio glass that took place in the United States, beginning in the 1960s with the small-scale experiments of such luminaries as Harvey Littleton and Dominic Labino, and culminating in the international phenomenon of Dale Chihuly. Traditionally in the United Kingdom it was Ireland and England that enjoyed a long-standing reputation for fine glassware that was founded in the seventeenth and eighteenth centuries.[8] The Scottish Glass Society was founded in 1979 and since that time more and more artists, both Scottish- and foreign-born, have emerged on the national and international scene. Due to the highly efficient network that exists among glass artists around the world, it is not surprising that Scottish glass today looks almost entirely international. Unlike the field of jewellery, one may be hard pressed to pick out the Scottish artists in a group exhibition of glass, which is in no way intended as a criticism. Glass has become a universally accepted art material, and has a very different recent history than many other of the crafts.

Alison Kinnaird works almost exclusively in flat glass (some is cast) which she engraves on the wheel, sandblasts, or acid etches, generally with imagery derived from her studies of the human figure. More recently she has been experimenting with fibre optics in combination with dichroic glass to create large-scale installations. Her imagery ranges from engravings of nude figures in timeless classical poses to studies of clothed figures captured in moments of casual and everyday movement. Her work is carefully layered to create a sense of space and depth belied by the flatness of the material. Her use of colour is often surprising – subtle gradations of light to dark in a panorama of soft hues. While the artist may refer to the colour of the Scottish landscape, the references are not blatant. A Scottish spirit, if one can be said to inhabit Kinnaird's work, must be found in the quiet grandeur of her forms and the intimacy of her processes.

Stephen Richard and Ray Flavell are also among the glass artists highlighted in *The Cutting Edge*. Richard's work can be placed somewhere between the flat glass installations of Kinnaird and the fully three-dimensional vessels created by Ray Flavell. Richard often brings the third dimension into his panels of glass in the form of extrusions or extensions that penetrate the planar space. Alternatively various patterns and motifs, mostly abstract shapes, animate the surfaces of his panels, which are sometimes free-standing sculptures. Ray Flavell has experimented with many other techniques of modulating the surfaces of his glass, and has also specialized in his personal revival of the 'Ariel' technique developed by Edvin Ohrstrom in Sweden in the 1930s, in which carefully controlled and shaped bubbles of air are trapped within the body wall of the vessel to create images or patterns. Flavell has been among the artists that have worked at the recently established National Glass Centre in Sunderland. This organisation, like the Pilchuck School outside Seattle, Washington, now serves as a powerful force in the international glass movement. As at Pilchuck, development of a personal visual vocabulary in glass is paramount; and while individual artists may bring a Scottish outlook to the making of glass, it remains a truly international medium.

Two of the artists working in glass have created new works for *The Cutting Edge*. Keiko Mukaide, who teaches in the Glass Department of the Edinburgh College of Art, has been a significant voice in British and international studio glass for several years. Asian born, Mukaide brings to glass a sensibility derived from an intimate relationship with nature, filtered through the lens of her Asian background. Landscape and natural elements are often references in her forms and in her installations. She has created large-scale installations at museums such as Tate St Ives, where she created a 55-foot long installation of shards of coloured glass, illuminated by a lighthouse lens. For *The Cutting Edge*, however, the artist will create an installation dealing with our sense of direction and our place on earth, as a metaphor for the human cycle of birth and death.

Mai Therese Ørsted, born in Denmark, exploits the liquid quality of glass, capturing growth and movement in a stop-motion action. Ørsted's forms are sensuous and organic, suggesting the irresistible power of ocean waves, or the delicate tapered curl of an unfurling leaf. While the artist uses colour in her work, it is carefully controlled and understated; some of her most successful works have been carried out in clear glass, allowing ambient light to interact with the forms and create subtle plays of shadow. Both Ørsted and Mukaide, foreign-born, are representative of the internationalism of studio glass today.

Textiles have had an ancient and revered history in Scotland; today there is a lot more happening in the field of fibre arts than tartan weaving and Shetland knitting alone. Makers are experimenting with cutting-edge materials and techniques to produce textiles and installations that are striking in their concept and imposing in their presence. Jilli Blackwood is a traditional practitioner of fibre art, in the sense that she is skilled in a wide variety of techniques such as dyeing, stitching and various forms of cutting. However, her use of these techniques is often radical – she slashes her woven textiles into frail fragments tentatively held together by the underlying structure. She subverts ideas about the functional nature of fabrics by producing wall hangings and wearables in which function may be acknowledged but is never in the director's chair. Gillian Cooper uses textiles to explore other aspects of contemporary culture as they relate to security and surveillance. Recently she has been using a computerized knitting machine to produce large works which incorporate digital images of human figures. While engaging the viewer to think of textiles such as blankets and throws as the ultimate security device, the images of surveillance that are depicted give Cooper's work a darker significance. If subtle subterfuge can be said to be a Scottish art-making behaviour, the works of Cooper and Blackwood are exemplary.

Noted basketry artist Lizzie Farey has dedicated much of her career to exploring the traditional basketry techniques of Scotland and other countries. She has been a painstakingly devoted disciple to the materials and processes that have made the history of basketry so rich. Starting as one of the earliest functional crafts, basketry has gone on to explore a realm of independent sculpture. Some of Farey's recent works have been outdoor woven 'structures' intended to suggest living spaces. For *The Cutting Edge*, Farey is continuing her explorations of material and space in work that incorporates natural materials and lighting technology to produce a hanging illumination.

Paper artist Rachel Hazell, known for her unique artist books which she writes, designs, illustrates, prints and binds, is among a growing number of international artists whose books are receiving attention from collectors and curators. She sometimes references nature in her work, as do many Scottish artists, but does so in a unique format. For example, a recent project was an interactive ice cliff of paper inspired by a trip to the Antarctic. For this exhibition she is making a book sculpture using sheet metal rather than paper. The shape of the book will be informed by the jagged edges of the Scottish landscape at large scale.

Textiles and metalwork come together in the work of Sara Keith and Roger Morris. Keith was trained in Japan, where she learned the demanding dyeing technique called *shibori*. While the technique has no history of use in Scotland, Keith has exploited the subtle colour gradations possible with *shibori* to evoke memories of the Scotland's landscapes. While she has produced wearable items, it is in her independent art pieces that Keith captures the attention of the viewer. Working with metalsmith Roger Morris, Keith will carry out further experiments with technology, using the nineteenth-century technique of electroforming to produce a collection of body adornments that merge the two mediums, and cross the barriers that separate traditional fibre from metalwork, and from the history of jewellery. A marriage between textiles and jewellery is also being arranged by Sarah Keay, who has produced neck and body pieces, inspired by floral forms, that are bobbin-knitted with enamelled wire. These works are intended to be large and dramatic – some between eight and twelve feet in length.

Sarah Taylor is among a small, but growing, number of textile practitioners

that are experimenting with new technologies, such as fibre optics. Taylor approaches her art as a researcher, studying the aesthetic potential of a new material, particularly when combined with a traditional technique. For *The Cutting Edge* the ancient world of weaving will be combined with new yarns and fibre optics to create work that exists in a newly-defined space between technology and art.

Jan Milne removes textiles one step further from the original context by printing onto acrylic sheets that are formed into pieces of furniture. One of only two furniture makers included in *The Cutting Edge*, the other being Mark Devlin, Milne's work speaks in a universal voice of contemporary design and fashion. Experimentation with synthetic materials is the hallmark of Stooshie Designs, who have created a Perspex panel to create layers of subtle colour and light.

The two faces of Scottish craft – the narrative and pictorial on one hand, and the abstract on the other – are expressed, respectively, in the work of ceramists Simon Ward and Sarah-Jane Selwood. Simon Ward creates objects that suggest that they may have some function, although few could be said to have practical functions. Often inspired by nature, Ward's branching, pierced, organic forms – often white porcelain with surprising bursts of colour, such as a brilliant red, on their interiors – recalls the veins and branches implied in Dorothy Hogg's jewellery. Like Peter Chang, Ward creates a landscape inhabited by alien species; his shapes are familiar and yet strange, recognisable and yet mysterious. Sarah-Jane Selwood comes at her material in a very different way. Her vessels are wheel thrown, cut and reconstructed. The severe angles and sharp edges are choreographed to produce a sense of dynamic movement. Her elegant black constructions of vessels within vessels evoke memories of the twisting energy of Frank Lloyd Wright's Guggenheim Museum building, or Frank Gehry's Bilbao Museum. Selwood represents the stern and disciplined aspect of Scottish craft that parallels the whimsy, humour and satire of many other artists.

Where does all this leave the viewer in terms of the Scottish identity in the world of craft? Clearly, all of these artists are part of an international community that is in constant communication with each other. In the 21st century it is very difficult for a working artist to exist as a recluse. New materials and techniques, new issues and concerns, new ideas and visions, continue to inspire artists globally; and while each may give an inflection of nationality to their work, the significance of the work is transmitted globally. Many of these artists do reference nature and landscape in their work, two elements that have inspired Scottish craft for aeons. It may also be interesting to note the parallel themes of nature and abstraction that seem to suggest schools of thought in Scottish art. Overall, there is a sense of modest good humour which I believe pervades many of the works. Without overstating the case, this is a national characteristic that I have lived with all of my own life, albeit long separated from the culture of Mull where my own ancestors probably made porridge, haggis, jokes, and – who knows – possibly jewellery.

ABOUT THE WRITER

David Revere McFadden is Chief Curator and Vice President for Programs and Collections at the Museum of Arts & Design in New York City. He served as Curator of Decorative Arts and Assistant Director for Collections and Research at Cooper-Hewitt, National Design Museum, Smithsonian Institution, from 1978 to 1995. For six years he served as President of the International Council of Museums' Decorative Arts and Design Committee. McFadden has organized exhibitions on decorative arts, design, and craft, covering developments from the ancient world to the present day, and has published and lectured extensively.

1 Conversation between author and Adamson, March 2002.

2 This wry and perceptive term was used by Roth in a presentation at the Oakland Museum of Art, Oakland, California in May 2004.

3 The research and writing of this essay is indicative of a sea change in critical writing practice. While not able to visit Scotland and spend time in the studios of these makers, I had constant access to them and their work by way of my computer.

4 Louise Butler (editor) with photographs by Shannon Tofts: *Scotland's Crafts* (Edinburgh: NMS Enterprises Limited – Publishing 2000). The publication contains essays by many authors on contemporary work by traditional crafts practitioners in tartan weaving, Harris tweed, Shetland and Fair Isle knitting, creels and skulls, etc. Each craft tradition was approached in the spirit set forth in Louise Butler's introduction as 'skills and goods that have their roots in Scotland's social, crafting and industrial past' (p. 1).

5 Op. cit., p. 101.

6 The work was featured in the special exhibition *Precious Statements* organized at Goldsmiths' Hall, London, 19 May to 1 July 2006, a two-person exhibition with Appleby and jeweller John Donald.

7 *100% Proof*, curated by Professor Dorothy Hogg, Edinburgh College of Art, toured 2005-06 venues in the United States and United Kingdom, following on from the earlier *100% Proof* exhibition in 2001.

8 Only recently has scholarly interest in early Scottish glass provided any insights into the history of the medium from the seventeenth century onwards. Among recent publications of note, see Jill Turnbull: *The Scottish Glass Industry 110-1750: 'To supply a whole nation with glass'*.

SCOTLAND'S ART SCHOOLS AND FURTHER EDUCATION COLLEGES WHICH RUN CRAFT AND DESIGN COURSES

Duncan of Jordanstone College
     of Art and Design
University of Dundee
Perth Road, Dundee DD1 4HT
Website:
     www.dundee.ac.uk/djcad/home.html
Telephone: +44(0)1382 388 219

Edinburgh College of Art
Lauriston Place, Edinburgh EH3 9DF
Website: www.eca.ac.uk
Telephone: +44(0)131 221 6000

The Glasgow School of Art
167 Renfrew Street, Glasgow G3 6RQ
Website: www.gsa.ac.uk
Telephone: +44(0)141 353 4500

Gray's School of Art
The Robert Gordon University
Garthdee Road, Aberdeen AB10 1FR
Website: www.graysartschool.co.uk
Telephone: +44(0)1224 263 600

School of Textiles and Design
Scottish Borders Campus
Heriot Watt University
Nether Road
Galashiels TD1 3HF
Website: www.tex.hw.ac.uk
Telephone: +44(0)1896 753 351

Cardonald College
690 Mosspark Drive
Glasgow G52 3AY
Website: www.cardonald.ac.uk
Telephone: +44(0)141 272 3333

Edinburgh's Telford College
350 West Granton Road
Edinburgh EH5 1QU
Website: www.ed-coll.ac.uk
Telephone: +44(0)131 559 4000

WEBSITES

Scottish Arts Council: www.scottisharts.org.uk
Craftscotland: www.craftscotland.org
Craft Ayrshire: www.craftayrshire.org

CRAFT ORGANISATIONS

Scottish Glass Society:
     www.scottishglasssociety.com
Applied Arts Scotland:
     www.appliedartsscotland.org.uk
Edge: Textile Arts Scotland:
     www.edge-textileartists-scotland.co.uk
Scottish Basket Makers Circle:
     www.scottishbasketmakerscircle.org
Scottish Potters: www.scottishpotters.co.uk
Scottish Craft and Furniture Makers Association:
     www.sfma.org.uk

PLACES TO VISIT

Aberdeen Art Gallery & Museums
Schoolhill, Aberdeen AB10 1FQ
Website: www.aagm.co.uk
Telephone: +44(0) 1224 523 700

The Dick Institute
1 Elmbank Avenue, Kilmarnock KA1 3BU
Website: www.east-ayrshire.gov.uk
Telephone: +44(0) 1563 554 343

Glasgow Museums
Kelvingrove Art Gallery and Museum
Argyle Street, Glasgow G3 8AG
Telephone: +44(0) 141 276 9599

Gallery of Modern Art
Royal Exchange Square
Glasgow G1 3AH
Website: www.glasgowmuseums.com
Telephone: +44(0) 141 229 1996

The Lighthouse, Scotland's Centre for
    Architecture, Design and the City
11 Mitchell Lane, Glasgow G1 3NU
Website: www.thelighthouse.co.uk
Telephone: +44(0)141 221 6362

National Museums Scotland
[including the former Royal Museum and
    Museum of Scotland]
Chambers Street, Edinburgh EH1 1JF
Website: www.nms.ac.uk
Telephone: +44(0) 131 247 4422

Bonhoga Gallery
Weisdale Mill, Weisdale
Shetland ZE2 9LW
Email:
    bonhoga-gallery@shetland-arts-trust.co.uk
Telephone: +44(0)1595 830 400

Gracefield Arts Centre
28 Edinburgh Road
Dumfries DG1 1NW
Website: www.web-link.co.uk/ gracefield.htm
Telephone: +44(0)1387 262 084

The Gallery
75/77 Main Street
West Kilbride KA23 9AP
Website: www.westkilbride.org.uk
Telephone: +44(0)1294 829 179

Dundee Contemporary Arts (DCA)
152 Nethergate
Dundee DD1 4DY
Website: www.dca.org.uk
Telephone: +44(0)1382 909 900

The Park Gallery
Callendar Park
Falkirk FK1 1YR
Website:
    www.falkirk.gov.uk/cultural/park/ park.html
Telephone: +44(0)1324 503 789

COMMERCIAL GALLERIES
WHICH PROMOTE CONTEMPORARY
SCOTTISH CRAFT

The Scottish Gallery
16 Dundas Street
Edinburgh EH3 6HZ
Website: www.scottish-gallery.co.uk
Telephone: +44(0)131 558 1200

Billcliffe Gallery
134 Blythswood Square
Glasgow G2 4EL
Website: www.billcliffegallery.com
Telephone: +44(0)141 332 4027

Open Eye Gallery
34 Abercromby Place
Edinburgh EH3 6QE
Website: www.openeyegallery.co.uk
Telephone: +44(0131) 557 1020

Orro
12 Wilson Street
Merchant City
Glasgow G1 1SS
Website: www.orro.co.uk
Telephone: +44(0)141 552 7888

EVENTS

WASPS studios: open days across Scotland
Spring Fling: open studio weekend, Dumfries and Galloway
Open studio events across Scotland

Dazzle exhibitions
Website: www.dazzle-exhibitions.com
Contemporary jewellery touring exhibitions

North Lands Creative Glass
Website: www.northlandsglass.com
Telephone: +44(0)1593 721 229
Annual glass conference and master classes

PUBLICATIONS

Very few publications have been produced focusing only on Scottish makers. However, the following list details some publications and exhibition catalogues in which Scottish makers feature.

Blackwood, J: *The Joy of Living* (Artbank [Scotland] Ltd, The Print People 2003).
Butler, L. (ed): *Raw Materials* (The Scottish Touring Consortium 1995).
Butler, L. (ed), with photography by Shannon Tofts: *Scotland's Crafts* (NMS Publishing Limited 2000).
Butler, L. (ed): *Develop Craft Ayrshire 2003-2006* (2006).
Cunningham, J: *Maker, Wearer, Viewer, Contemporary Narrative European Jewellery* (2005).
Dalgleish, G: *Collection 2000* (The Scottish Gallery 2000).
Dalgleish, G, A Game, R Miller and C Rew: *Silver from Scotland* (Aberdeen City Council/The Scottish Gallery).

Fillis, I and A McAuley: A *Craft Businesses in Scotland: A study* (Scottish Arts Council/Scottish Enterprise 2002).
Game, A and E Goring: *Jewellery Moves: ornament for the 21st century (*NMS Publishing Limited 1998).
Game, A, E Goring, and C Rew (eds): *Fired with Colour: Aspects of Enamelling in Britain* (The Scottish Gallery 2000).
Goring, E: *Edinburgh comes to Clerkenwell* (Lesley Craze Gallery [London] 2005).
Greenhalgh, P. (ed): *The Persistence of Craft* (A & C Black 2002).
Hamilton, L. and P Scott (eds): *The Plate Show* (Collins Gallery/University of Strathclyde, Glasgow 1999).
Harding, J, J Harris and P McMorris: *Burbidge, Telos Portfolio Collection* (Telos Art Publishing 2004).
Hogg, D and A Game: *100% Proof, A Second Generation of the Distillation of new work in jewellery and silversmithing from Scotland* (published by flow 2005).
Moncrieff, E: *Creation: An insight into the mind of the modern silversmith* (The Goldsmiths Company 2004).
Patrizio, A: *Elemental Traces* (Royal Botanic Garden Edinburgh 2000).
Swann, P and C Rew (eds): *Malcolm Appleby* (Malcolm Appleby 1998).
Vaizey, M: *Dorothy Hogg 10 Year Retrospective 1994-2004* (The Scottish Gallery 2004).

EXHIBITIONS

Peter Chang: A visionary
Taideteollisuusmuseo (Museum of Art and Design, Helsinki, Finland 2000).
Digital Perceptions, Collins Gallery, University of Strathclyde, Glasgow, exhib. catalogue (2006).

Making Weaves, The Basketmakers' Art (National Museums of Scotland, Edinburgh).

Glorious Obsessions, Scottish Indigenous Crafts Today (Scottish Arts Council 2000).

Gordon Burnett (The Robert Gordon University/ Monash University 1999).

Building Bridges Scottish Arts Council Support for Crafts in Scotland 1993-2003 (Scottish Arts Council 2003).

The Millennium Collection for Bute House (The Incorporation of Goldsmiths of the City of Edinburgh 2000).

Jerwood Applied Arts Prize catalogues (Crafts Council, London 1994 onwards).

10 Years Crafts (The Scottish Gallery 1996).

Katie Horsman MBE 1911-1998 Memorial Show (The Scottish Gallery 1999).

Scottish Glass Now, 10th Anniversary of the Scottish Glass Society (Glasgow Museums and Art Galleries 1989).

Elements of Change, Contemporary Ceramics from Scotland (Scottish Touring Consortium 1994).

Source, Scottish applied arts inspired by museum objects (National Museums of Scotland, Edinburgh).

Gifted, Five Years of the Inches Carr Scottish Craft Awards (National Museums of Scotland, Edinburgh 2002).

Jack Cunningham Journey (The Lighthouse, Glasgow 2000).

Jack Cunningham on the Line (The Glasgow School of Art 2003).

100% Proof A distillation of new work in jewellery and silversmithing in Scotland (flow 2001).

The Scottish Glass Society Exhibition 2006 (Collins Gallery, University of Strathclyde, Glasgow 2006).

Clay in Bloom (Scottish Potters Association 2004).

Contained Spaces, The World at her fingertips (Collins Gallery, University of Strathclyde, Glasgow 2004).

GLOSSARY

CANNEL COAL

A type of bituminous coal that burns brightly with much smoke.

DICHROIC GLASS

Dichroic is a multi-layer coating placed on glass using a process known as thin film coating. Originally created for the Aerospace industry, dichroic glass is increasingly being used by glass artists.

ELECTROFORMING

A process which coats material with partial or minimal layers of fine metal. A metal skin can be built up on any surface that has been rendered electro-conductive through the application of a substance containing metal particles and the use of controlled electric charges in a plating bath.

FIBRE OPTICS/OPTICAL FIBRES

Thin flexible glass or plastic fibres which transmit light signals, normally used in tele-communications. Optical fibres consist of an inner core and an outer cladding; they omit a cool light and do not omit ultra-violet light (UV) or conduct electricity.

LASER-WELDING

Heat-free process using fine lasers which enables surfaces of metal to be fused together. Allows extreme precision with tiny laser beams fired into the surface of metal. The laser beam can be adjusted down and up to within fractions of a millimetre and the voltage of the laser beam can also be adjusted. Enables makers to combine work with metals and combustible or fragile materials that cannot be exposed to heat.

LED LIGHTING

Light Emitting Diodes as a light source. LEDs have a much longer life than conventional light bulbs and also use less power. This makes them more economical. They can be used indoors and out, as normal lighting, or in design and craft work.

MONOFILAMENT

Monofilament line is a thin string made from a single fibre. Because of its strength and low cost, most fishing line is made from it. Monofilament is made by melting and mixing polymers and feeding the end product through tiny holes, forming the line, which is then spun into spools of various thicknesses.

SHIBORI

Shibori is a Japanese term for methods of dyeing cloth with a pattern by binding, stitching, folding, twisting, or compressing it before the textile is dyed. Some of these methods are known collectively in the west as tie-dye. There are many different terms for the individual shibori techniques.

WATER-JET CUTTING

A machining method that uses a jet of pressurized water containing abrasive powder for cutting glass, steel and other dense materials.